Angelina Jolie

First published in Great Britain in 2006
by A Jot
26 Thurloe Street
London SW7 2LT   UK

© A Jot 2006

ISBN 1-905904-00-2
     978-1-905904-00-6

Design: Darren Morris

Printed and bound in Poland
by Bialostockie Zaklady Graficzne SA
Al. Tysiaclecia P. Polskiego 2
15-111 Bialystok

Angelina Jolie

Brandon Hurst

ajot

CONTENTS

A JEROME HELLMAN · JOHN SCHLESINGER Production

DUSTIN HOFFMAN JON VOIGHT
MIDNIGHT COWBOY

BEST
PICTURE
1969

INTRODUCTION

Sometimes a movie is not much more than the music. If you could only remember one thing about *Midnight Cowboy* [Schlesinger, 1969], it would be Nilsson's 'Everyboy's Talkin''. Of course, in this case, the film matches the score, not least with two fabulous performances from Dustin Hoffman and John Voight – Angelina Jolie's father – which deserved more than just Oscar Nominations. Thirty years after its release, a reviewer wrote tellingly of it: 'A landmark film in its unflinching descent into the New York gutter, *Midnight Cowboy* remains emotionally, technically and cinematically stunning today.' The poignant 'Everybody Talkin'' also remains a classic, which has been covered numerous times.

Everybody's talking at me
I don't hear a word they're saying
Only the echoes of my mind

People stopping staring
I can't see their faces
Only the shadows of their eyes

I'm going where the sun keeps shining
Thru' the pouring rain

Going where the weather suits my clothes
Backing off of the North East wind
Sailing on summer breeze
And skipping over the ocean like a stone

8

Angelina Jolie was born some six years after the release of the film that had made her father a bankable star. A year later her parents separated and she was brought up by her mother; her relationship with her father was fraught and, as she often calls it, 'stormy'. In 1997, during a lull between the storms, she gave a joint radio interview with her father (they were in different studios) in which he recalled her birth:

> This is a momentous occasion for me, because the last public conversation we had was when you were born. You don't remember it, but when you emerged from your mother's womb, I picked you up, held you in my hand, and looked at your face. You had your finger by the side of your cheek, and you looked very, very wise, like my best old friend. I started to tell you how your mom and I were so happy to finally have you here, and that we were going to take great care of you and watch for all those signs of who you were and how we could help you achieve all that wonderful potential God gave you. Your mom and I made that pledge and everyone in the room started crying. But we weren't crying; we were rapt in each other's gaze.

It was a peculiar thing to say to his 22-year-old daughter who knew that while her mother was pregnant with her he had been involved in an affair with an actress called Stacey Pickren.

Angelina Jolie

And that six months after Angelina was born, her mother kicked Voight out of their family home. Nonetheless, from the moment she was born, there was an awareness in Jon that his daughter was going to be 'different' and how all the 'energy' that she always displayed was going to have to find a home.

Angelina certainly did turn out to be different, leading a life that does skip over the ocean like a stone. Occasionally she has sunk, other times she has been wiped out, but always she gets back up to 'going off' those waves.

She is that very rare thing in human beings: a free spirit. Which is why she touches people's hearts. They see in her someone who is not trapped in anything except her own choices to be honest and to act on what she believes in.

Angelina Jolie is no great thinker, not the greatest beauty nor the best actress around, but she is a great human being. She has made lots of mistakes, but she has learnt from them and always she keeps going thru' the pouring rain to where the sun keeps shining.

This is her story.

CHAPTER 1
EARLIER YEARS

EARLIER YEARS

Jon Voight was born in 1938 in Yonkers, New York, to a Czeck father and an English American mother. His classic Slav features he undoubtedly took from his father as he did his ox-like stature. He grew to 6'4" and is a powerful man who could have become a professional athlete. In fact, his own father was a professional golfer, although he could not compete because of incurring a back injury when he was young. However, he coached and taught all three of his sons to play at club level.

Jon was the middle brother but all three of them made their mark in their particular field: James (Chip Taylor) the youngest became a songwriter, penning the simple but popular rock'n'roll standard 'Wild Thing', which Lennie Hendrix virtually made his rock anthem. The oldest, Barry, became a professor geoscience at Penn State University.

The Voights were a religious family and took their Catholicism seriously. Jon attended Archbishop Stepinac High School, then went to Catholic University of America in Washington, D.C. where he graduated in art. Despite his natural talent for drawing and painting, from an early age he had expressed a desire to act. At High School and University, he took an intense interest in drama productions and, on graduating and after spell in the army, he worked and studied at acting in New York.

Angelina Jolie

Around this time, he married an actress Lauri Peters whom he met while they were both studying under the acting legend Sanford Meisner at the latter's Neighbourhood Playhouse. Lauri was also a singer and dancer – a trooper who while highly respected in the industry never went beyond co-starring with Cliff Richard in *Summer Holiday* (1963). Voight and Peters did not have any children, divorcing after five years – although the actual marriage lasted only two. During this apprenticeship, he met and became friendly with Dustin Hoffman who was on the same track as him.

Meisner had a massive influence on American acting and pioneered a fresh approach to method acting. He spoke about the goal of acting as 'living truthfully under imaginary circumstances' and that 'the foundation of acting is the reality of doing.' He was an inspirational teacher in conveying this and, in 1997, when he died at the age of 91, the tributes just poured in. Aside from Voight, Meisner taught Jeff Goldblum, Robert Duvall, Diane Keaton, James Caan, Steve McQueen, Grace Kelly, Gregory Peck, Joanne Woodward, Allison Janney, Mary Steenburgen, Eli Wallach, James Doohan...

The playwright Arthur Miller once said of him: 'He has been the most principled teacher of acting in this country for decades now, and every time I am reading actors I can pretty well tell which ones have studied with Meisner. It is because they are honest and simple and don't lay on complications that aren't necessary.'

Earlier Years

Angelina Jolie

After her acting career finished, Lauri Peters returned to New York theatre and also taught acting. In 1993, with Sanford Meisner's blessing she founded the Meisner Extention at NYU (Undergraduate Drama, Tisch School of the Arts). As he had many other actors, Meisner left an indelible mark on Voight. Indeed, he left him with a vocation.

Meisner: 'Life beats down and crushes our souls and good acting, good theatre reminds everyone they have one, a soul – at least the type of theatre that I am interested in. Actors have the opportunity to literally change people's lives if they work on the material that stands for something.' Throughout his career, Voight has tried to play parts that stand for something and has tried to bring to them the same truth and honesty that they would have if they were real.

In 1966, he read a novel by James Leo Herlihy, which had come out the previous year. Called *Midnight Cowboy* it charts the odyssey of a naïve Texan dishwasher, Joe Buck, who goes to New York to make his fortune by servicing those rich women who were 'begging for it' and 'paying for it' too. There he hooks up with a street-smart hustler with a limp who reinforces his delusions and, while vaguely acting as his pimp, skins him alive. However, after being ripped off, he sees Rico Ratso Rizzo by chance and, in the aftermath of forlorn attempt to get back his money, they form a friendship. The two lost outcasts, hustling for a buck in the underlife of the city, stop behaving like they were in a dog-eat-dog world. For a short time, they reclaim their humanity.

Earlier Years

Jon was impressed by the book and, as he knew that Herlihy had already had one book turned into a movie, was alerted to its potential when he heard that John Schlesinger was to make the movie. He rang Hoffman and said that he must audition for the Ratso part as he could play it to perfection. He also put himself forward as Joe Buck but, although Schlesinger booked Hoffman, he rejected Voight. However, Keil Martin, the actor whom he cast as Buck was under a studio contract and had to turn down the part. Voight remembered 'flying to New York, got a meeting with the casting director, the director and the screenwriter and finally got the part. It changed my life and gave my father a great sense of relief, because he realised that I was finally going to make money as an actor.'

The film turned out a timeless masterpiece, which Hoffman credits to Voight's sense of humour. The interplay between Ratso and Buck certainly had an element of vaudeville but John Barry's score and use of the 'Everybody's Talkin'', Adam Holender's hand-held camera-work, Schlesinger's feel for the subject... In his 60s, Voight looked back and conceded, 'I am still very impressed with that work: it stands the test of time. The high-water mark of my career...'

He said of it in a comment that could easily have been written by Meisner, '...the power of it's statement in terms of compassion and the expression of truth, and standing in people's shoes who are needy and without certain equipment to face life was a statement that was very high-minded, a highly moral statement.

Angelina Jolie

I'm a person who wants to express things in an authentic and true fashion, and if I've made a mistake by getting too graphic at certain times, well maybe I have, but it's always been in the pursuit of some deeper truth.'

It turned Voight into an overnight star. It is in 1970, when he was making *Catch-22* that he had an affair with 20-year-old model-cum-actress named Marcheline Bertrand. Marcheline's family originally came from French Quebec but settled in Chicago, where she was raised with her brother. Her mother is part Native American (the Haudenosaunee tribe) descent and this comes through in the looks of both Marcheline and Angelina: the long face, the straight dark hair, the Mongoloid slightly slanted eyes.

Marcheline studied acting at the Strasberg Institute in New York and worked intensively in the theatre, while supplementing her income with some modelling work. She was a proper model… not a 'glamour model'. Her acting never took off commercially in that unlike Voight she never made the transition from stage to screen or, indeed, even the small screen. Her best TV role was in a February 1971 episode of 'Ironside', a series that featured Ramond Burr as a detective in a wheelchair. Nonetheless, she worked constantly in the theatre and had a genuine passion for acting.

When she met Voight, he was coming out of one of his hippie phases and she inspired him to get back on the work track. He gave up grass and sleeping around for her. In a way, she

Earlier Years

turned out to be his only love, even though he didn't know it at the time. And by the time he did know it, it was too late.

They got married in December 1971 in New York. For all his fame and standing in an industry where self-promotion can be even more important than one's acting, Voight has rarely courted publicity. Marcheline is far more dismissive of the publicity hoopla of Hollywood than him, so her determination to keep their private life out of the spotlight and flashbulbs was quite uncompromising. The wedding was attended by family and friends and received hardly any media attention. They lived together in New York both pursuing their acting careers before moving to Los Angeles.

Marcheline Bertrand and Jon Voight, 1973

Marcheline Bertrand and Jon Voight, some 6 months before Angelina was born

Their first child, James Haven, was born on 11 May 1973, then, two years later, Angelina Jolie. Marcheline took care to give her children middle names that they could use as surnames if they decided that they didn't want to be associated with the fame of their father. Jacqueline Bissett and Maximilian Schell were Angelina's godparents.

However, by the time, she gave birth to Angelina, the marriage was already threatened by Voight's womanising. Jon, then, oscillated between his Catholicism and fidelity in marriage and the drugs-cum-free love philosophy of the counter-culture 60s, which was concentrated on the West Coast where he spent a lot of time working. He now embraces a kind of spiritual polytheism in those days but, as his friend Dustin Hoffman once noted, it was a bit more complicated: 'Jon is a strict, lapsed Catholic boy who has to pay for his sins in guilt.'

Earlier Years

Around the time of Angelina's pregnancy, he had begun dating a wacky bit actress called Stacey Pickren, who belonged to an evangelical free love cult called the Children of God. Stacey is one of those women who could never be a prostitute as she'd enjoy it too much and feel like she should pay the man not vice versa. She wanted a lot of sex...a lot more than any one man could give her.

Jon decided that he would go with this as he was caught up with the notion of confronting the hang-ups of his upbringing. At one stage, when she was pregnant with Angelina, Marcheline came downstairs unexpectedly and saw her husband kissing Stacey Pickren. She went back to their bedroom and began shaking with shock and, as she thought she would have a miscarriage, called an ambulance. She forgave him and they continued living together but the affair with Stacey continued.

The final straw in their marriage was when he turned up at their home wearing an amulet of Stacey's cult around his neck. When Angelina was six months old, she decided to leave Jon Voight and she left Los Angeles, too, settling in Manhattan, NY. He began living with Stacey. The Voights did not formally divorce until 1978, when Marcheline won custody of the children.

She gave up acting in order to bring up her two children but Voight was less than generous with maintenance payments and while James and Angelina's childhood was not impoverished it was circumscribed. They continued living in Manhattan where

Marcheline met a 31-year-old fringe actor named Alan Mezo. They fell in love and he moved into her apartment. Mezo was effectively Angelina's father for nearly three years.

Marcheline, then, decided to take her family to Beverley Hills and Mezo went along with them. He didn't find work and Marcheline eventually decided that it would be best if he returned to New York. Jon Voight was still living with Stacey Pickren and, given that Marcheline was living with Mezo, he was difficult with money.

In the late 1980s, Marcheline wrote a letter Mezo, which some 17 years later he sold to the *New York Post*. It provides one of the few windows that we have on Angelina's early teens. In the letter Marcheline expresses sorrow for dropping Mezo: 'Perhaps I was just in too much emotional pain back then to appreciate you. The truth is, I never would have made it through that difficult time without you.'

Mezo told the *Post* that he '...cared for them all so much. But we met just at the wrong time. She was still married to Jon Voight. She told me that he had not treated her well, and I think there were other women involved. She found it so painful and it made it hard for her to trust another man.'

Nonetheless, Marcheline wanted Mezo to know about the children who were now 13 and 15: 'Angelina is 13. She is studying to be an actress and a playwright... My children have grown up quite splendidly. Jamie is 15 and aspiring toward a career in film marketing and distribution. He also loves basketball!'

Mezo said of Marcheline when he sold the letter and some accompanying pictures: 'She was so kind, so caring, so generous – she was honestly like an angel. Her children meant everything to her. Of all the people I have known in my life, she was easily one of the best. And Angie has got that from her. That is why she does so much work for the U.N. and wants to adopt needy children. I think all the good things you see in Angie, she got from her mother.'

Voight did give one interview in 1979 to *Photoplay* magazine ['Jon Voight: A Rare Interview'], in which he spoke about his relationship with Pickren. He said of their open relationship: 'I think that once you say everything is wide open, you're going to get into a little difficulty. But if that's what you have to do, that's what you have to do. But she's free to do what she wants to do and I'm free to do what I want to do. There are no rules, and there's no mortal sin as far as that's concerned. No great sin that can't be looked at and understood. If someone needs something, someone should be allowed to have it, as far as I'm concerned.'

Yet he admitted to the interviewer that he still succumbed to the green-eyed monster when Stacey had sex with another man: 'I can't handle the pain. I'm trying to work it out. I don't want Othello to be taking over my personality, you understand. I'm trying to live with the aspects of myself that I think are more valuable.'

Angelina Jolie

Despite his two busted marriages and the abandonment of his Catholicism, Voight still celebrated and extolled the ideal of marriage: 'The idea of two people getting together and making a commitment, if they can get there, I think it's very beautiful. It's very touching, always. It's the reason we cry at weddings, because what we're doing, in a sense, is saying something that's impossible. Marriage is wonderful because people say I love you forever. It's a magnificent statement, and so courageous and powerful and beautiful; and I'm very moved by it. I'm glad people attempt it.'

Moved by this courageous, open statement, the interviewer then asked him if he would risk another shot at marriage this time with Stacey. He replied in a roundabout way that he wouldn't: 'I believe I have a lot of affection and a lot of love for an awful lot of people. I believe I can fall in love with quite a lot of people. And I have certain respect for my responsibilities. I take it one day at a time. I'm trying right now to be less possessive of the things I love and people in my life – and with my children, too. It means that I'm trying to make it work with Stacey. I'm focusing on her. If she need somebody or I need somebody along the line, I can't say well that's lousy, and it hurts me so deeply I would leave you forever…although I may do that.'

Impressed with Jon's honesty and compassion Will Tusher, the interviewer, ended his article: 'It's really true: Jon Voight is one person who cares about absolutely everybody.' Presumably, everybody included Jon too.'

Earlier Years

Voight got an Oscar for best actor in the schmaltzy *Coming Home* [1978] but with this under his belt it gave him the clout to virtually do his own movie. He chose a mob comedy and it provided Angelina with her first part on screen. *Lookin' To Get Out* is a mob comedy that Voight wrote, although much of it was actually improvised on set. Angelina plays Tosh, who is cast in the movie as his ex-girlfriend's daughter. She was six when it was filmed – mainly in the M-G-M Grand Hotel. Also in the film with small parts are Stacey Pickren and Marcheline Bertrand!

Angelina, 6, in
Lookin' To Get Out

Angelina Jolie

In this eminently forgettable comedy, Angelina delivers a handful of lines in the few brief minutes she appears on screen at the end of the film. Stills of her scenes show that, even at six, she already displayed the beginnings of those delightful lips – known in Hollywood as 'a pair of Grade A DSLs' – that would later become one of her trademarks.

Some of her earliest memories are about the acting lessons her father gave her, evidently keen that she should follow in his footsteps. 'My earliest memories are of my brother, Jamie – your son – pointing the home video camera at me and saying, "C'mon, Ange, give us a show!"' she told him in the same interview. 'Neither you or Mom ever said, "Be quiet! Stop talking!" I remember you looking me in the eye and asking, "What are you thinking? What are you feeling?"' Whilst her relationship with her father remains unresolved, it is clear that at least part of her does appreciate the time he spent with her back then, and the skills he taught her. 'That's what I do in my job now – I say, "OK, how do I feel about this?" And I immediately know, because that's how I grew up,' she said.

She showed an early determination to be different though, in that she collected snakes and lizards. She also liked performing and attracting attention, wearing glittery clothes drawn from the glam-rock of 80s rock'n'roll. Then, in 1986, when she was eleven, her mother decided to go back to Los Angeles where the family stayed permanently.

Earlier Years

As puberty beckoned she became a bit of an ugly duckling with braces, glasses and long uncoordinated limbs. Her big lips and slightly poppy eyes added to her muppet-like look, for which she was ragged by her school friends. Adolescence was not a happy period.

The home movies she mentioned show her dressed in high heels, with sequined tops and tassels. However, she would be the first to emphasise that this phase of her life was short-lived. It wasn't long before girlie turned to Goth and she discovered a whole new set of far more enduring influences. 'I bought lots of leather,' she said. 'Black and red leather. Dog collars. Things like that. When other little girls wanted to be ballet dancers I kind of wanted to be a vampire.'

Her ambitions at this point tended less towards the cinema than the crematorium: at the age of 12, her aspiration was to become a funeral director. She even began to take a mail-order course to learn the trade, and to this day still has a copy of the 1987 Funeral Service Institute Handbook in her home to prove it.

The interest in death has never gone away, but she is quick to contextualise what some see as excessive morbidity. 'Because I am a bad girl, people always automatically think that I am a bad girl, or that I carry a dark secret with me or that I'm obsessed with death. The truth is that I am probably the least morbid person one can meet. If I think more about death than some

Angelina Jolie

other people, it is probably because I love life more than they do.'

Back in LA and attending Beverley High School, Angelina was not one of the rich and privileged kids she remembers meeting there. Life took a turn for the worse. She was very self-conscious about herself – something that has stayed with her ever since, despite her self-evidently stunning looks and frequent Most Beautiful accolades. 'I just think I'm kind of goofy,' she said. 'I've always been one of the boys growing up.'

She was skinny, wore braces and glasses and didn't measure up to the standards of the Beverley Hills girls, who teased her about her appearance. 'I always hung out with the guys more when I was growing up. I never really had girlfriends,' she said. 'I'm not soft and emotional, so it's probably easier to approach me as another guy because the girl side of me is very private.'

Earlier Years

CHAPTER 2
Teens

TEENS

In her early teens, Angelina's difficult family circumstances and repeated knock-backs destroyed her self-confidence. As a result, she started to suffer from insomnia, eating disorders and even began to cut herself. 'I collected knives and always had certain things around,' she said in an interview for *CNN*. 'For some reason, the ritual of having cut myself and feeling the pain, maybe feeling alive, feeling some kind of release, it was somehow therapeutic to me.'

As far as real therapy goes, Angelina never rated it very highly. 'My film roles are my therapy,' she claimed in later years. Her one experience of it dates to her teenage years when it became obvious to her teachers that something was wrong. 'I went to therapy for extra credit when I was in high school,' she said. 'That's Beverley Hills High for you – you can get credit for therapy! The doctor wanted to make everything about the fact that my parents divorced. The doctor was probably going on about my father and mother while I was doing acid on the weekends and bleeding underneath my clothes.'

Angie was never under the impression that the return of her father would solve all her problems; she actually used to pray that her parents would not get back together. They never did, and the following years saw many ups and downs in their precarious relationship, before she finally severed ties with him completely. 'I don't hate my father,' she told *The Mirror* last year. 'I don't blame him for divorcing my mother or having affairs. I just don't want to dedicate one more tear...or have to watch my mother cry one more time. I don't respect the way he treated my family as I was growing up.'

At 14 she dropped out of school and fell heavily into drugs and alcohol. 'I think a lot of the problems I had growing up were because I didn't leave my environment enough,' she recalled some years later. This was after her charity work had given her a fresh perspective on life. 'If you don't get out of the box that you've been raised in, you won't understand how much bigger the world is – and what is truly real.'

BLOOD, BLADES, BOYS AND BODY ART

'I know I present myself as many things. I'm very sexual, yet I've always been monogamous. I feel both masculine and feminine. I understand that side of men that encompasses the lone person. I have the restless spirit of a man.'

One of the things that has come to define Angelina is her voracious sexual appetite. This is clearly more hype than reality. In 2003, after she adopted Maddox, she told the *Scottish Daily Record*: 'I can count on less than the fingers of one hand the number of men I've slept with.' On screen, she has played Lara Croft, the vixen archaeologist of the *Tomb Raider* films, whose curvy, sexually-charged incarnation from the world of pixels to that

Teens

of celluloid has excited many a game-geek around the globe to a state of near frenzy. But whilst this, and other film roles, have been considerably aided by her compelling physique and bad-girl allure, it is no exaggeration to say that the biggest intrigues have come off-screen: the boyfriends, the girlfriends, the marriages, the open displays of affection and frank discussions of fringe sexual practices... Frequently titled the Most Beautiful Woman in the World, it is no surprise that she attracts considerably more than her fair share of interest, both on the dating front and on the part of an increasingly captivated and envious press and public. (A survey by Blockbuster movie rental chain found her the woman that most men would like to date on New Year's Eve.)

Angelina's reputation has arisen from her habit of being outspoken and entirely unashamed about her sexuality. In this area, as in every other, the secrecy so avidly pursued by most other celebrities is simply not her style; she does not pursue or even seem to want it. Her candour can occasionally seem shocking – though it is perhaps more disturbing to the tabloid press, in that it robs them of the need to search out the stories for themselves. It's easier simply to ask. 'I'm extremely honest, and I pride myself on it,' she said. 'I don't try to be shocking. I'm playful, and I know when something I'm saying is maybe shocking, but it's just the truth. I never wanted to be scary to people or upsetting to people. I simply want to live the way I need to live.'

Angelina has a 'no regrets' attitude to her love life, whether in long or short-term relationships, and makes it a rule not to

Angelina Jolie

dwell on the past. 'I don't believe in guilt,' she said. 'I believe in living on impulse as long as you never intentionally hurt another person, and don't judge people in your life. I think you should live completely free... I would like to be open with the public. I would like to not keep secrets or be careful when I talk. I don't want to have to plan things. I want to be outspoken. I want to say my opinions and I hope they're taken in the right way. I don't want to stop being free. And I won't.' Although she has apparently been on very friendly terms with Jonny Lee Miller since their divorce, she claims that she has never deeply mourned the end of a relationship.

Renowned for pushing the boundaries, in and out of the bedroom (one magazine rather uncharitably – and with some exaggeration – referred to her as 'pansexual') she has become a Hollywood poster-girl for the sexually liberated. 'Honestly, I like everything, boyish girls, girlish boys, the heavy and the skinny,' she told *Elle* magazine. And yet, she retains a sense of perspective and is disturbed by the promiscuity she sees in younger people today. 'Kids are doing a lot of weird things really young these days and they're getting very promiscuous. I'm an adult woman who uses safe sex and has healthy relationships with people I care about,' she says: the bar for her is not the number of partners but the quality of relationship.

'Yeah, I have been married twice and now have these great friends who have crossed over into being lovers,' she says. 'And there is no reason why there can't be more than one.'

Teens

Angelina playing guitar at 10 years old, then clockwise at 15 (note how those DSLs were already developed and remain untouched by the plastic surgeon). Next, at 16, as she began modelling. Finally in suspender belts at 18.

Angelina Jolie

She freely attributes this easy-going attitude to her early teenage years, when she struggled to cope and began to rebel by drinking, taking drugs and having sex. 'I've had a lot of unusual things in my life that have made me how I am,' she states. 'I lost my virginity when I was 14. He was my first boyfriend at the time. I wanted to be promiscuous and was starting to be sexual.' Marcheline, her mother, was pretty relaxed about the situation. Whereas many parents would be shocked to know what their children are up to, she allowed her daughter's boyfriend to move in. 'We lived like a married couple for two years,' Angelina recalls. 'He lived in our house with my mum and my brother, so it wasn't like we were on our own.'

Now, she appreciates her mother's understanding. 'I got lucky,' she said. 'We were in my bedroom, in my environment, where I was most comfortable and I wasn't in danger.' Marcheline's acceptance during those years is one of the things to which she credits their close friendship now. 'I could always talk to my mum if there were any problems – she was more connected and aware of what was going on than most mothers.'

It is also to this first relationship that her well-documented interest in S&M can be traced. 'You're young, you're drunk, you're in bed, you have knives – shit happens,' she once said in a throwaway line. 'I got knives out and had a night where we attacked each other. It felt so primitive and it felt so honest...' Although the full story was more complicated than that, as with all her spiel to the press, there was only a grain of truth in her recollections. In

Teens

fact, this was part of the pattern of self-harm that began around the time the family moved back to LA. Characteristically, even for such a personal subject, she has spoken openly about this in interviews. 'I started having sex and sex didn't feel like enough and my emotions didn't feel like enough. My emotions kept trying to break out. In a moment of wanting something honest I grabbed a knife and cut my boyfriend, and he cut me.'

Self-harm is a hidden but surprisingly common problem. Angelina is one of a number of celebrities who have spoken about it. Still, this was one aspect of her relationship that she couldn't discuss with Marcheline. 'I had to deal with not telling my mother, hiding things, wearing gauze bandages to high school,' she remembers. It started a pattern that would last for many years, only ending when she adopted her Cambodian son. 'Before Maddox, nothing seemed real and honest enough. That's why I put myself in danger. That's why I literally used to cut myself to feel some pain and why, in many of my early relationships, I encouraged my lovers to be violent. I have a scar on my jugular to prove how dangerous and stupid those times were.' Angelina has been roused to fury when fans come up to her and show her the scars they got when they tried to emulate her.

'I was like a real punk kid, and I was going out of my mind,' she says of that time. 'But by the time I was 16 I wanted to be alone and free.' Those two years taught her a lot about herself, including the fierce independence and self-sufficiency that has marked her relationships and charity work in recent years.

Angelina Jolie

She recalls how she toughened and began to push people away, avoiding displaying her emotions and even pushing away physical contact. 'Something just happened,' she says. 'I asked my Mum and she said that one day I just stopped wanting to be hugged. And it's not just hugging: I don't cry a lot either. Early on in my life I saw people crying and saw that it never accomplished anything, so I figured, what's the point? My first boyfriend cried a lot and it was just a load of high drama that I could do without.'

'Looking back, I think I was probably not good for him,' she said in an interview with *Rolling Stone*. 'He was somebody that I wanted to help me break out and I would get frustrated when he couldn't help me. Which was when the knives came in – he'd be asked to cut me or I'd cut him. When you need somebody to get aggressive with you and it's not in their nature...' When they broke up, Angelina also moved out and found an apartment of her own, a block or so down the road from Marcheline.

In a 2004 interview with *Allure* magazine, Angelina explained a little more to a (largely) uninitiated public what her interest in S&M was really grounded in. 'S&M sex can be misinterpreted as violence,' she said. 'It's really about trust. I like to push boundaries, both emotional and sexual, with another person. That's when I've felt the sexiest. I've been in both submissive and dominant roles because I want more.'

The link with trust is illuminating for someone so self-sufficient;

Teens

it seems that Angelina keeps a minimum distance between her and even her closest friends and companions. She doesn't fully hand over control, not trusting even her lovers.

In an interview with *Elle* Magazine, she elaborated. 'I need someone physically stronger than me... I am always on top. It's really unfortunate. I am begging for the man that can put me on the bottom. Or the woman. Anybody that can take me down. I've never been tied up. I have a feeling the person that does it will be the One. I think that's what I'd like.' In a more recent interview with the *Mail on Sunday*, she admitted, 'I don't think I'll ever trust anybody 100 per cent. I have great friendships and relationships, but even the people that you know love you might not always do things that are going to help you.'

It seems that Angelina keeps a minimum distance between her and even her closest friends and companions. Yet, it is patently obvious that Angelina knows how to give good copy. For a woman who can count the lovers on the fingers of one hand, she clearly talks much more sex than she does.

Her love of tattoos also dates to this time. Today, she sometimes cannot remember how many there are (there are regular additions, and occasional changes as out-of-date tattoos are altered or lasered off). Many psychologists see a link between self-harm and tattooing; the release of endorphins characterises both and, in the same way that cutting can become habitual as a coping mechanism, some people become psychologically addicted to getting tattoos. Of the many designs on her body, some recall the difficulties and angst of her teenage years. There is the Latin motto, Quod me nutrit me destruit ('What nourishes me destroys me') on her lower abdomen. This has become a slogan for those with eating disorders and other destructive lifestyles. There is also the Tennessee Williams quote, 'A prayer for the wild at heart, kept in cages' – which she had inked on her left arm. A later design, the Japanese character for 'death' on her left shoulder, has since been covered by a Buddhist prayer for her adopted son.

Angelina links her tattoos to her gradual process of development. 'Usually, all my tattoos came at a good time,' she said. 'A tattoo is something permanent, when you've made a self-discovery, or something you've come to a conclusion about.' Many of them are markers for significant events in her life and are linked to her relationships and children. (Although this is not always the case.)

On one occasion whilst visiting the Netherlands, she got drunk and made an impulsive decision to get another one. 'I dropped my pants in a tattoo parlour in Amsterdam,' she hazily recalls. 'I woke up in a waterbed with this funky-looking dragon with a blue tongue on my hip.' Whilst tattoos can be removed by lengthy and painful laser treatment, it is often easier to have them covered by another design. This is the origin of the large Latin cross on her stomach. 'I realised I made a mistake, so a few months later I got a cross to cover it. When my pants hang low, it looks like I'm wearing a dagger!'

Teens

'I have a lot of tattoos,' she admits. 'It's not typical for an actress, but I don't think it's abnormal that someone who spends her life in other skins wants to claim her own by marking things on it that matter.'

Her love of body art has occasionally caused problems, as they often have to be covered for her acting roles. She is not against nudity in films, but like most actresses is not happy about the

Angelina's back tattoos

Angelina Jolie

way soft porn is becoming the Hollywood norm. Ironically, her tattoos often mean that while a script may involve nudity, when faced with the problems of using make-up to cover up her body art, directors tend to have second thoughts about her stripping off.

Of course, people do the same thing for different reasons and tattooing and body piercing have become quite fashionable among women. Clearly there are all manner of motives at work... not least copycatting someone like Angelina Jolie. It is difficult not assume in her case, however, that her tattooing developed from her self-mutilation impulses and may well have been a way of channelling this into something less harmful.

CHAPTER 3
A SHOOT-UP STAR

A SHOOT-UP STAR

When she broke up with her boyfriend and moved out into her own place, things gradually started to come back together for Angie. She resumed her studies and finally started to get some call-backs for her modelling auditions. She ended up working for Finesse Model Management and even travelled to London for photo shoots. Some of her early work also includes a number of music videos. Amongst others, she featured in the Rolling Stones' 'Has Anybody Seen My Baby', Lenny Kravitz's 'Stand By My Woman', and Meatloaf's 'Rock and Roll Dreams Come Through' ('he was a genie with pointy ears and I was a runaway,' she remembers).

Her earlier experiences as an aspiring but unsuccessful model gave her a fresh perspective of the business. Today, Angie is a down-to-earth woman with no airs and graces, and without the pretensions that she could so easily have acquired. She may be famed for her stunning looks, but she has a healthy attitude towards them. 'I have to do photo shoots for magazines, and I kind of think, "Okay, do you want to put that much make-up on me?"

She once said, 'We are setting an example for what we think is beautiful, and I just don't understand it.' Although her fame rests partly on those looks, she is the first to admit what a shallow

Angelina Jolie

approach that can foster. 'You might never find out that you're useful for all the right reasons – and not all those stupid things that people tell you you're useful for.'

In LA, Angie signed up with the Met Theatre Group and soon found acting work. Her first proper film outing in over eleven years (other than in some of her brother's student productions) was in the sci-fi thriller *Cyborg 2: Glass Shadow*. The movie was set in 2074 and features the 17-year-old Angie as a cyborg seductress, programmed to infiltrate a rival company's headquarters by any means at her disposal and then detonate. 'When I saw it, I threw up for three days,' reported Angelina about her debut. 'My brother held me and I went back to school and didn't want to work again.' The appalling film was not an auspicious beginning to her career. However, it did highlight the fact that, even at the age of 17, Angie had been recognised for the sexual allure she represented to the audience. Unfortunately her next major work, *Without Evidence*, fared little better. Although she featured heavily in the advertising, and her face no doubt drew a reasonable proportion of its audience, hers was a minor role and she did not actually appear on the screen until an hour into the film. It was not enough to rescue the movie, which fans and critics alike promptly consigned to the same mental bargain basement as *Cyborg 2*.

As yet, she was not sure of the direction she wanted to take in life, though acting certainly had its attractions. 'I loved some kind of expression…I'm very good at trying to explore different

A Shoot-Up Star

emotions and listen to people and feel things.' The uncertainty meant that she frequently struggled with depression, and even found herself contemplating suicide at times. Buying an apartment in LA triggered one of her blackest moments, as it highlighted the fact that she really did not know her direction in life.

'I didn't really want to live,' she told *Rolling Stone*. 'So anything that was an investment in time made me angry…but also I just felt sad. I sat on the floor and cried, because I was trying to pick out carpet color and I thought that I wasn't going to live to put it in. I couldn't sleep. I always felt like I wanted to burn harder or go faster than everything around me, always. I lived very, very much inside.'

Despite her misgivings, she quickly found more work, this time on the small screen and in a couple of shorts. The bizarre 2-minute *Mr Viril* movies feature smouldering performances from Angie, clear proof of her potential and things to come. Her first role of any real magnitude was that of computer whiz Kate 'Acid Burn' Libby in the techno-thriller *Hackers*, and it heralded many changes in her life. She would be acting alongside up-and-coming talent Jonny Lee Miller.

Beauty and the Brit

'I have always developed deep ties with actors who have played alongside me. I always fall in love,' Angie said after filming wrapped for *Mr. & Mrs. Smith* early in 2005. In fact, all of her major relationships and many of her dalliances (whether merely rumoured or otherwise) have begun on the set.

Jonny Lee Miller – a member of the Natural Nylon (Jude Law & co.'s production company) Primrose Hill set who rose to superstardom as the pasty-faced heroin addict Sick Boy in the cult film *Trainspotting* – was to become Angelina's first husband. This was also her first relationship since moving out of her mother's house. 'I had my first boyfriend when I was 14 and then I didn't sleep with anybody until I met my first husband at 19,' she said. 'It's funny that's shocking to people.' Despite her reputation, Angelina has regularly had long periods of voluntary celibacy; intimacy, when it happens, is strictly on her own terms.

She and Jonny first met in 1995 on the set of *Hackers*. Miller's grandfather, Bernard Lee, was well known for his role of M in the first dozen Bond films, though his own credits up to that point included only a string of TV roles, and nothing more significant that a year-long stint in the BBC1 soap *EastEnders*. Angelina, too, was all but an unknown in the industry. Although *Hackers* didn't do so well at the box-office, it raised both of their profiles and pushed them both a vital step closer to the elusive 'breakthrough' role that heralds mainstream success. Another factor in raising their profile was their relationship, which by providing the press with plenty of column inches also put them in the public eye.

Three years her senior and at a roughly similar point in his career, Jonny was smitten. Notoriously bashful (Jonny doesn't like to see his own films, and once claimed, 'I can't approach women, I'm not really like that'), he has always been reticent about how their relationship blossomed. 'It was great,' he told *Interview* magazine in a rare comment about their experience together on and off the set. 'We got on very well. She's very beautiful – that didn't slip by my attention. But that's all I can say, really. I can't go into anything else. I don't mean to be rude, but that's the rule I have. I feel shy about it.' Angelina, naturally, was more forthcoming. 'We met while filming *Hackers* and I always fall in love while I'm working on a film. It's such an intense thing. And I've always been at my most impulsive when English men are around. They get to me. When I was 14, I visited London for the first time and that's when I discovered my problem.'

For a while, it looked like the romance that had begun on the set would end there. She and Jonny had been close when working together on *Hackers*, but immediately after filming wrapped Angelina didn't want things to continue. He had been her first lover since she was 16 and the emotional intensity was difficult to handle. They took a step back from each other and, briefly and temporarily, lost contact. In the relatively short time before they got their relationship back on track, Angelina began a much-publicised relationship with another one of her co-stars.

Jenny Shimizu

'I consider myself a very sexual person who loves who she loves, whatever sex they may be,' Angelina told *Cosmo* in 2004. 'If I fell in love with a woman tomorrow, would I feel that it's okay? Yeah.'

Hackers wasn't well received by the critics, and it didn't turn much of a profit at the box-office either. But it did gain quite a cult following when it was released on video, no doubt partly because Angelina's sultry looks did wonders for the image of actual computer hackers. In any case, the film served its purpose and very soon, more opportunities started coming her way. She starred in two largely forgotten films, *Mojave Moon* – a comedy about a road trip – and *Love Is All There Is*, a modern-day *Romeo and Juliet* remake.

Foxfire, a film about the friendships between five wayward teenage schoolgirls, was Angelina's next job and the third film she was to make that year. Among the cast was the Japanese-American actress Jenny Shimizu, whose better-known credits include a topless modelling shoot for *CK One*. The sexual undercurrents in the film spread off the set, with Jenny and Angelina beginning a long-term relationship that (Jenny maintains) continued over the course of the next decade. 'I realised that I was looking at her in a way that I had looked at men,' Angelina told *Cosmo* in 2004. 'And it was great, and it was a discovery…. It was never something I was looking for. I just happened to fall for a girl.'

Whilst Jenny had always been attracted to women 'from the minute I could distinguish the sexes,' developments initially came as a bit of a surprise to Angelina. 'I was surprised when I suddenly found myself having the feelings for this woman that

A Shoot-Up Star

I had only previously felt for men. I wanted to kiss and touch her,' she told *The Mirror* in 2003. All the same, it was something she took in her stride, later deciding that it was no big deal. 'I thought the point of being an artist was to express yourself,' she says simply.

Not wishing to drive a wedge between them, Jenny was initially restrained in talking about their relationship to the press and denied that there was anything between them. Since Angelina confirmed it herself, Jenny has given lengthy interviews about the subject. In an interview with Showbiz Reporter, she described how they met. 'During breaks in filming *Foxfire* I got to sit down with this person and spend two weeks with them, meeting them and talking with them before anything got sexual. I felt intense emotions and I felt intense emotions from her. From that minute on we hung out together.' Jenny has stressed that their relationship was predicated on far more than the physical, and that there has been an enduring connection between them. 'I actually felt like I was caring about someone much more than just simply having sex. And I didn't feel there was a straight girl that I was just bedding and she was going to freak out the next morning.'

'I had never been so tender with another person as I was with her,' she said. 'We had established such a nice relationship that I felt this girl would have me back, no matter what. I knew this person would be loyal and wonderful to me. Our relationship only got closer the minute that we had finished being together.

Angelina Jolie

She's a gorgeous woman. She's a very dominant personality. Once she displays love for you, she wants to know how much you care about her.'

Angelina's relationship with Jenny, which started when she was 19, has lasted longer than any of her others. After they finished *Foxfire* together, the two stayed in touch. 'For a while back then, if Angelina called, I'd drop everything and join her wherever she was in the world,' Jenny told *DIVA* magazine. 'Angelina and I had a really wonderful relationship that lasted many years. I was dating her while she was seeing other people – she was that type of person; wonderful and open.' In an interview with *The Sun*, she even spoke about going to Angelina's house in Cambodia and exploring the jungle with her.

'I wanted people to know that I'd been with a woman,' Angie said. 'I spoke about it because I had discovered something wonderful and I thought people should know my experience was very real, very normal.' All of this has turned Angelina into something of a poster-girl for bisexual women, a group who are bizarrely under-represented in Hollywood. Whereas lesbianism seems perfectly normal – consider the lesbian roles and actresses in the industry – bisexuality is still not entirely accepted. The unspoken axiom seems to be that a bisexual woman is one who has yet to discover her true identity, and is therefore not properly accepted by either the straight or the gay camp. Angelina's ongoing affair with Jenny has made her into an icon for bisexual women the world over, particularly as she is so at home with herself. 'They're right

A Shoot-Up Star

to think that about me, because I'm the person most likely to sleep with my female fans, I genuinely love other women. And I think they know that,' she once said.

All of this must have been slightly disturbing to Jonny Lee Miller when he and Angelina got back in touch and started dating again. Although the ongoing affair with Jenny made things awkward when he visited her on set, Angelina dealt with it in typically direct style. 'We were already sleeping together when I met Jonny while on *Foxfire*,' Jenny remembers. 'She told both of us how she felt and we all went out to dinner one night. She was honest – that's how she's been her whole life.' She was at pains to make it clear that, although the three of them got on well enough together, that was as far as it went. 'We didn't have a threesome. I'm not really into that. It was a friendship the three of us had,' she said. 'But there wasn't very much conversation with Jonny. I think he was very threatened by me.'

TYING THE KNOT

Jonny apparently wasn't threatened enough by Angie's bisexuality to stop him pursuing a relationship with her. She, too, chose to be with him. Although she married Jonny, Angelina has hinted that her interests were divided at the time. 'I probably would have married Jenny if I hadn't married Jonny,' she said after their eventual divorce.

It seemed to their friends that the quiet Brit and the often loud and outlandish American were a strange couple. In interviews, however, both have opened windows onto the other's public image. 'English men appear to be so reserved, but underneath they're expressive, perverse and wild,' said Angelina, speaking initially about her time with Jonny. (And then, 'All the insane moments of my life have happened with English men.') Jonny, too, witnessed a side of her personality that many had previously missed or ignored. 'Angelina's image is of a wild, crazy, femme fatale,' he said. 'But she's not. She's a very nice, big-hearted girl. It wasn't extraordinary at all that we were together.'

Jonny, who hit the big-time with his role as a junkie in *Trainspotting*, was a calming influence on her. 'I have done just about every drug possible, cocaine, ecstasy, LSD and, my favourite, heroin,' Angelina told *The Mirror* in 1996. 'Although I have been through a lot of dark days, Jonny has helped me see the light.' As far as celebrity pairings go, this one was kept surprisingly quiet. Jonny's references to the relationship went about as far as admitting that he'd been 'involved with an American girl who lives in LA'. After a whirlwind cross-Atlantic romance, the couple decided to tie the knot on March 28, 1996 – even before *Hackers*, the film that brought them together, was released. It wasn't exactly a traditional ceremony, although anyone familiar with Angelina's taste in clothes and philosophy would be hard-pushed to see her in the fairytale meringue dress. All the same, the symbols and ceremony of their commitment raised eyebrows even in eccentric Hollywood.

The wedding itself was a small, civil ceremony in Los Angeles.

A Shoot-Up Star

Only Marcheline and Jonny's best friend were invited. Her father, with whom she was still on speaking terms at the time, could not attend; he was filming *Mission Impossible*. Instead of the usual morning suit and waistcoat, Jonny wore black leather. Angelina shunned a veil and went for a pair of black rubber trousers instead. Her white blouse had his name written across the back of it, in her own blood (which, she was careful to impress, she had extracted herself from her arm with a clean surgical needle). 'It's your husband,' she said by way of explanation. 'You're about to marry him. You can sacrifice a little to make it really special.' Jonny moved to LA to live with her, where they shared their bed with Harry Dean Stanton, her albino corn snake.

'It was a great opportunity to explore other worlds and to move and work in Los Angeles with a purpose,' Jonny said about the move. 'But being nuts about her also had something to do with it.' Within a short time, the glitz and pressure of Hollywood would unfortunately wear thin and prove to be a major problem between them. Jonny soon realised that he was happier in London, and married life turned out to be a big shock for Angelina, too. For someone who had been so independent, suddenly coming as one half of a celebrity package was tough to get used to. She had always felt that she stood in her famous father's shadow; now, she was not only the daughter of a film star, but the wife of one, too.

'It was weird to immediately be married, and then you kind of lose your identity,' she complained. The feeling was particularly acute as the couple were promoting *Hackers* together at the time. 'You're suddenly somebody's wife. And you're like, "Oh, I'm half of a couple now. I've lost me." We went on some morning show, and they threw rice on us and they gave us toasters. I was thinking, "I need to get myself back."' Initially over the moon with her new husband, it wasn't long before the cracks started to appear. 'I am so self-sufficient that I didn't know how to let a man be a man,' Angelina has said of that year with Jonny. 'Or how to commit to buying a house together. I could never even be on the same insurance.'

To this day, Angelina remains on good terms with her first ex-husband; so much so, that there are periodic rumours fuelled by pap shots of the couple in public that they are going to get back together. But she recognises that it was a very difficult time in her life and a big part of her just wasn't ready for that kind of commitment. 'I wasn't even a good friend because I was just absent...I'd go for drives and disappear or go film something and be in hotels forever and not do anything, not have friends, not visit, not hang out. I couldn't calm down and just live life,' she admitted.

They both had separate filming schedules, and it would be a while before she learned to balance work with the rest of life. 'I am not present enough, physically or emotionally, in relationships to get serious,' she said, some years later after the break-up of her second marriage. 'It's not fair to the other person that I'm so busy with my career and that I'm often distant even when I am with someone.' It is clear that – despite her claims never to have regretted the end of a relationship – her marriage to Jonny was one that she has misgivings about finishing. 'I wanted to commit to Jonny,' she said, several years after the two went their separate ways. 'But he deserved more than I was prepared to give him at the time. I'd like to tell Jonny I love him. But I think he already knows.' They separated after only a year, in 1997, though the divorce wasn't finalised until two years later in early 1999.

'I didn't want to divorce him, but I had to, you know?' she said. There was no custody battle over dependants; Harry Dean Stanton had already flown the nest. Some time earlier, both Angelina and Jonny had been leaving for separate filming jobs. They were unable to find anyone willing to kill the mice that Harry fed on, and Angelina decided that the only sensible thing to do would be to bring the snake to an early end.

In the event, she found she couldn't do it herself. Instead, she phoned the vet who had taken care of Vlad, her pet iguana, when she first became too busy with acting commitments to look after him. Given that this was the second time around, the vet placed a condition on his cooperation. 'If you promise me you'll never get another pet, I will take Harry and find him a home,' he said.

'I assume he was kidding,' said Angelina later. 'I just tried to think what was for the best, and realised most of the time that being

Angelina Jolie

with me was not the best thing for a pet.'

Breaking Through

While their marriage played out, both Jonny and Angie went on to bigger and better things. *Foxfire*'s reception had been mixed – some critics slammed it, others loved it for and despite its perceived faults – but Angelina's performance was usually singled out for praise. 1997 brought with it two made-for-TV movies: *True Women* and the biopic about the racist governor of Alabama, George Wallace. In the latter, Angie played Cornelia Wallace, his second wife. She won a Golden Globe and received an Emmy nomination, both for Best Supporting Actress. This was her first critical recognition and a major part of her 'breakthrough' into mainstream cinema. Immediately after the TV films, *Playing God* brought her back onto the big screen, this time with some better-established stars such as David Duchovny, the *X-Files*' tousled and much-loved Agent Mulder, and Timothy Hutton, whose performance in 1980's *Ordinary People* had made him the youngest ever Academy Award winner.

Angie's role in *Playing God* was the dangerously flirtatious girlfriend of a rich mobster, Timothy Hutton. At times unbelievable, the film nevertheless managed to brighten the careers of all of the major actors. It also provided Angelina's next boyfriend. Once again, she found that the experience of playing someone's love interest on screen had off-screen consequences. She had separated from Jonny by the time *Playing God* was released, but it was not until she eventually filed for divorce in February 1999 that she and

A Shoot-Up Star

Timothy got together. The relationship was brief, but apparently intense; one of Angelina's many tattoos is a letter 'h' on her wrist which dates from this period. (Fortunately, her brother's surname – Haven – begins with the same letter, so there was no need for laser removal treatment in this instance.)

Angie's breakthrough was cemented by her next film. *Gia* was another TV biopic, this time of the 1970s lesbian fashion model, Gia Marie Carangi. Gia's compelling story was one drug abuse, broken relationships and, ultimately, her early death from AIDS in 1986 at the age of 26. Angie was in good company: Faye Dunaway was playing Wilhelmina Cooper, Gia's agent and surrogate mother.

Whilst her looks suited her to the part of the supermodel, the role demanded far more depth than this and was the first real test of her acting skills. Angie threw herself into the part with a will, drawing on her own experiences to make her character as realistic as possible. After all, this was a character with whom she could identify. 'My first instinct was probably a lot of people's,' she told the *Boston Herald.* 'You think, "Oh, she's a model. She's cool, she's got attitude, she's tough…" – all of those things. But the real essence of this story is that she's like every single one of us who just needed desperately to be loved and understood and felt that she had some purpose on this planet.'

In fact, for a while she was worried that the shared details in their lives would prove too problematic. 'Initially I was afraid I would identify too much with Gia, that we had too much in common with similar issues and frustrations,' she said. 'In the end, I learned some pretty strong things about myself, that I'm a lot softer than I thought I was.'

The result was met with outstanding critical acclaim, including a second Golden Globe and a second Emmy nomination. Typical amongst the reviews was that of *Variety* magazine, which called the film 'a mesmerizing tour de force for lead Angelina Jolie': 'Two elements drive the film into the stratosphere...there is 22-year-old Jolie – a relative newcomer whose most visible role to date was her Golden Globe-nominated turn as Cornelia Wallace in TNT's *Wallace*.' As Gia, she is a multifaceted revelation, shifting from coquettish to nasty to violent to contrite with a breathtaking believability. The passion with which she inhabits the role is a spectacle in itself; it doesn't hurt that she's also a spectacular beauty.'

Angie didn't hold back, even having her head shaved for the scenes at the end of the movie, where Gia is dying of AIDS – despite the fact that she knew this would restrict her acting opportunities in the immediate future (bald actresses being in limited demand). Her dedication also spelled the end of her failing marriage. The method acting she had studied at the Lee Strasberg Theatre Institute required that she stay in character in between scenes. She was separated from Jonny but still on good terms, apparently without having given up all hope of reconciliation. She realised that her work ethic effectively made it impossible for him to relate to her. She refused to phone him. 'I'd tell him, "I'm alone; I'm dying; I'm gay; I'm not going to see you for weeks,"' she remembers.

MAKING A SPLASH

Her performance was enough to win another Golden Globe award, as well as a Screen Actor's Guild award and Emmy nomination. By this stage, Angie had realised that acting offered the outlet she needed to express herself. 'Acting is not pretending or lying,' she said. 'It's finding a side of yourself that's the character and ignoring your other sides. And there's a side of me that wonders what's wrong with being completely honest.'

At the 1998 Globes ceremony, dressed in a hand-sewn Randolph Duke gown, she coolly accepted her award on the stage. Then, showing the opposite side of her personality, she jumped in the fountain.

One of the stranger episodes in her life dates around this time, when her success appeared to be beckoning her into a career in the movies. Exhausted after *Gia*, and uncertain of the direction she wanted to take next, Angie immersed herself in a combined film studies and writing course at New York University and stopped acting for a while to concentrate on her college work. In her own words, she felt that she had 'nothing left to give.'

It was a very lonely time for her. 'I didn't have close friends any more and the city just seemed cold and sad and strange, and the subway rides – everything that was kind of romantic about New York just got very cold for me.'

Not for the first time, she decided that she would be better off dead. In contemplating her suicide, however, she ran into a snag. She knew that her mother and brother would feel responsible for her death, and she didn't want them to suffer that. 'With suicide comes the guilt of all the people around you thinking that they could have done something. With somebody being murdered, nobody takes some kind of guilty responsibility,' she said.

The ingenious solution she came up with was to hire a hit man to do the job for her. In an interview with *Rolling Stone*, she discussed meeting with a man (a 'friend of a friend') who, she had been advised, was involved in that line of work. She even started to plan financially for the event. Believing that it would cost tens of thousands of dollars, she began to put money aside gradually so that no one would be able to trace it after she was dead. 'It's so weird and so complicated and so completely insane…so strange,' she recalled. 'And so like a fucking movie.'

When she told the hit man what she wanted him to do, instead of taking her money and doing the job, he suggested she reconsider. 'This person said very sweetly to me, he made me think about it for a month. And by a month other things changed in my life and I was surviving again.' Soon afterwards she gave up her studies at New York and returned to film-making.

A Shoot-Up Star

With the critical success of *Gia* behind her, there was no question that further roles of significance would come her way. Despite the hiatus and self-doubt, she showed a ferocious work ethic. In the spring of 1997 she worked on *Hell's Kitchen*, a crime thriller, and the romantic comedy *Playing By Heart* came next. Both films, which came out the next year with *Gia*, opened up new frontiers to her.

In 1997, her father Jon Voight interviewed her about her recent projects – a curious dynamic that offered perspectives of both actor and parent. 'I've been learning a little more about the side of myself that enjoys being a light,' she said. 'I remember when I used to dress all in black and you'd say, "Just be pretty, hold your head up, be proud. Be a pleasant person and don't cover yourself so much with all your darkness, your need to be a little crazy." Now, I have nothing against anything I've been in before, because I love all sides of me, but I have been experimenting more with that lovely woman side. In this age of feminism, I would hate for the whole gentlemen and ladies thing to be lost.'

She also spoke of some of the difficulties she was experiencing in being cast; some of her earlier roles as an uninhibited siren were threatening to put her in a pigeon-hole that was undesirable and professionally dangerous. 'I'm having to do a lot just to keep my clothes on and not be cast in girlfriend roles,' she complained. 'Some women will say, "I don't want to be a man – I want all the opportunities I can get as a woman." Women have a certain sexuality, and I think their bodies are beautiful and I'm not embarrassed to explore that in a film. But there are things you get offered that are vulgar and violent.'

At this stage in her career, Angie and her father were still on good terms. She credited him with much of her acting skill, and finished the interview with the words, 'I love you too, Daddy.'

A Shoot-Up Star

[above] Some of Angelina's more risque shots
[btm opposite] Her favourite painter, Egon Schiele,
made something of a speciality of painting nude women

Angelina JOLIE

CHAPTER 4
THE BEVERLEY HILLBILLIES

THE BEVERLEY HILLBILLIES

Angie's next big picture was the comedy drama *Pushing Tin* – a slang term for what air traffic controllers do. The film featured a rivalry between two controllers, played by Billy Bob Thornton and John Cusack. Angie played Billy Bob's beautiful wife who, naturally, becomes part of the rivalry and the object of Cusack's affection. At the time they met Thornton, who is 20 years Angie's senior, was best-known for his role in the 1996 film *Sling Blade*, which he wrote, as well as both directed and starred in.

Thornton is something of an all-round entertainer. He sings and writes songs with Dwight Yoakam, and since being told he was too ugly to act at the beginning of his career, diversified into script-writing to give his bow another string. Billy Bob is famed for his several marriages and various idiosyncrasies. He has often confessed his Obsessive Compulsive Disorder, which manifests itself in – amongst other things – an intense phobia of antique furniture and certain types of cutlery (which he self-deprecatingly and humorously references in some of his films). Like most OCDers, he is very particular about the cracks on the sidewalk.

In short, he was not the kind of man you would expect a stunning actress with the world at her feet to fall for. Always one to surprise her friends, not to mention the intrigued public, the

Angelina Jolie

eccentric and wild Billy Bob was exactly where Angelina next set her sights.

Their often-recounted first meeting in a lift occurred at a time after Billy Bob had divorced his fourth wife and was living with actress Laura Dern ('God bless her. I hope she's so happy. I want her to be happy. But it was over. That's all,' Billy Bob told *US Weekly*). For her part, Angelina was still dealing with the aftermath of her split from Jonny and trying to figure out what needed to change to make things work next time. When they met, neither of them was in much of a position to start something new, though they both remember the spark they felt.

Billy Bob recalls their first meeting. They had recently both agreed to work on *Pushing Tin*, although filming had not yet begun. Arriving in Toronto, one of the filming locations, they happened to step into the same lift together. 'I said, "I'm Billy Bob – how are you doing?" and then we came out of the elevator, and I just remember… you know, wanting something to not go away? Wishing the elevator had gone to China,' he told *Rolling Stone* magazine in 2001. 'It's like a bolt of lightning. Something different happened that never happened before.'

Angelina's recollections were a little more dramatic. 'Something went wrong with me in the elevator,' she said. 'Chemical. I really walked into a wall. It was the elevator. I kind of knocked it as we were both getting out. He got into a van and he asked me, "I'm trying on some pants – you want to come?" And I nearly

The Beverley Hillbillies

passed out. All I heard was him and taking off his pants. I just said "no". And I went around the corner and sat against a wall, breathing, thinking, "What was that? What the fuck was that? Jesus, how am I going to work?" I was just confused. I became a complete idiot.'

The friendship swiftly developed as they filmed *Pushing Tin*. 'We became friends in a really amazing way,' said Angie. 'I just wanted to be near him all the time. And I missed being around him when work was over.' When the excuse to be around each other was gone, it looked like the hope for anything more would be over before it had even begun. 'We talked on the phone every once in a while. But there was nothing we could do,' she said. 'We couldn't entertain the idea of it becoming anything else because the situation wasn't available. I was actually forced to be in a room with him a lot because of different business functions, and it was so hard. I almost couldn't talk to him sometimes. I'd wonder why I felt so much for someone I hardly knew. My life completely changed when I met him-just knowing there was someone like him alive. But without him, a part of me always felt empty.'

Billy Bob eventually took the initiative to put things right. 'There was a day when I knew that my life needed to change and I walked – no, I drove – to her and said, "Can you meet me in five minutes? We can be together now." And we have been ever since. In retrospect, you find out you knew everything. You think back and know you were desperate for someone you couldn't be with. You shut off a part of yourself because if you let yourself feel it, you won't be able to live with it.'

'I felt like I came alive that night,' she told *US Weekly*. 'And every day and every second since, it's been more intense and better and more beautiful. I look at him and nothing else matters. We just talked that night. We talked and looked at each other.' They managed to keep things quiet for a while, but the deal was sealed in the public's eyes when Angelina was spotted with a new 'Billy Bob' tattoo on her left arm. He also had the first of several tattoos to reference Angelina done in 2000 – a magic mushroom (a nod to his favourite band) with 'Angie' written on it, inked on his left calf.

BONE COLLECTOR

In the gap after *Pushing Tin* before the two of them finally got together, Angie went from strength to strength on the screen. Many fans consider *The Bone Collector*, her next film, to be Angie's definitive breakout performance, the one which established her as a mainstream actor to the public and ensured that she would be around for many years to come. Her role was that of a rookie cop investigating a series of murders, acting as the eyes and ears of a quadriplegic forensics genius (played by Denzel Washington). Although the part once again made use of her stunning looks and figure, thanks to the recent awards and nominations she was increasingly gaining recognition for her acting abilities too. She was now highly capable of marshalling emotions from her own considerable

The Beverley Hillbillies

life-experiences and translating them to performances in front of cameras. 'The first time Angelina and Denzel met, she had almost a shyness with him,' director Phillip Noyce told *Harper's Bazaar* back in 1999, 'and I knew that she was going to transfer that shyness to her character.' The test audience agreed, to Denzel's surprise. 'The focus group couldn't stop raving about Angelina,' said Noyce. 'Finally, Washington couldn't resist shouting out, "And what about Denzel? Don't you think he was great?"'

Janeen Schreyer, Angie's make-up artist for the film, remembers how her looks occasionally caused problems for her character: she was just too photogenic at times. In one scene, she dons a wetsuit in what is supposed to be the dirty and unglamorous line of duty. 'She has a darling figure, so the thing on her, it looked like a sex suit,' Schreyer told *Harper's Bazaar*. Directors' expectations also differed from Angie's own. She saw herself as the essentially down-to-earth and unpretentious actress; they often saw her as the face from the model shoots. 'They "Just want you to be you,"' she said. 'But not the you you. The other you. The person on the cover of the magazine.'

That sentiment seems to have carried across to the reviews. Critics weren't so impressed, citing the plot's many gaping holes, well-worn clichés and gratuitous suspense devices. Angie came in for regular mention, of course, but was usually singled out for special mention for being too beautiful, despite the make-up department's best efforts. 'Jolie is a captivating young actress (heck, most of us would be happy to watch a two-hour loop of her balancing her checkbook) but even she can't make us believe that she gave up a lucrative modeling career to become an underpaid cop,' wrote Vanessa Vance. 'In her various get-ups she looks like a stunning teenager dressed up in daddy's uniforms.' As is so often the case, the critics' opinions didn't ultimately matter. Audiences – like the focus group – loved the film, which grossed over three times its $48 million budget.

Whereas *Bone Collector* was a critical failure but a popular success, *Girl, Interrupted* marked a critical high point in Angie's career. The title is a reference to a painting by Vermeer: *Girl, Interrupted at her Music*. The film, which is about the experiences of a young woman in a mental hospital in the 1960s, is based loosely on the memoirs of Susanna Kaysen (played by Winona Ryder). Following a drugs-and-alcohol suicide attempt at the age of 18, Kaysen was encouraged to commit herself to a psychiatric facility. On doing so, she was diagnosed with Borderline Personality Disorder and found herself confined in the hospital for two years. Angie played the supporting role of Lisa Rowe, one of Susanna's friends in the hospital. Needless to say, the range of emotions and situations she was called upon to replicate presented an enormous challenge. It was one she rose to superbly.

Angie never met the real Susanna Kaysen. 'She hasn't decided to be in contact with me,' she told the *Boston Herald*. 'I think she's lying low and will contact me when all of this blows over

The Beverley Hillbillies

with you. She had a child and it's a boy and probably around my age now. I think she's in New York and maybe just now settling after going through a lot.' In fact, Kaysen criticised the film for diverging too much from her diaries. The result was a movie that some people claimed ended up glamorising mental illness – again, a hazard of hiring one of the world's most attractive women to act in it.

Angie had to rely largely on her own feelings and experiences for her performance. Here, her acting training and wild-child past came into its own. 'Jolie is emerging as one of the great wild spirits of current movies, a loose cannon who somehow has deadly aim,' wrote critic Robert Ebert. James Berardinelli was as complimentary, but more effusive. 'Angelina Jolie...shines like a supernova, radiating flamboyance. It's an electric performance that energizes every scene in which she appears, recalling but not imitating Jack Nicholson's turn as Randle P. McMurphy in *Cuckoo's Nest*. This is top-notch acting that avoids the cliché pitfalls, and, although Ryder is equally as good, Jolie's work is the kind that gets recognised at awards time.'

Berardinelli hit the nail on the head. Angie's performance, her best to date, far upstaged lead actress Winona Ryder's and won her a slew of awards. She received her third Golden Globe award in as many years, and another Screen Actors Guild award. Marking the pinnacle of cinematic acclaim, *Girl* also won her the 2000 Academy Award for Best Actress in a Supporting Role. (She also managed a Teen Choice Award nomination for Choice Hissy Fit, a less-than-coveted award for the ability to throw a good temper tantrum on screen.)

GIRL, INFURIATED

It was her first and, to date, only Oscar. (She does remember attending the ceremony once before with her father, as a 12-year-old.) As a child, she remembers seeing her Voight's Oscar – she was only three when he brought it home for Best Actor in a Leading Role in 1978's *Coming Home*. 'I never held an Oscar before,' she said. 'It's quite heavy. My dad's mother had his in a goldfish bowl or something on the mantelpiece and you grow up thinking it's this strange thing in grandma's house. I don't remember much about it.' Voight was 39 when he won his; Angie was 15 years younger, and perhaps this is the occasion when she decisively stepped out of his shadow and finally started to be recognised on her own terms, not as the talented child of a bigger star.

At the time, she was filming *Original Sin* down in Mexico with Antonio Banderas. After receiving her award, she flew straight back south. The director, Michael Cristofer, as well as many of his film crew, had also worked with her on *Gia*. Cristofer and Banderas were mindful of Angie's crash-and-burn response to her first major success, the depression she suffered on finishing *Gia*, and were keen that she did not repeat it. Shortly after she fell asleep in the early hours of the morning, she was awakened by the sound of the Mariachi band that Cristofer had hired. Cristofer had organised his crew to meet at her trailer, and

The Beverley Hillbillies

as she got out to find out what was going on, each of them handed her a rose.

Despite their best efforts, the aftermath of the Oscars saw Angie embroiled in yet another controversy, this one far-fetched and poisonous even by the usual standards. She had attended the ceremony with James Haven, her brother (like Angie, he had long since ditched their father's surname, using his middle name instead). In her acceptance speech, she said 'I am so in love with my brother right now!' She also planted a kiss on his mouth which, along with her other affectionate behaviour, became the subject of much comment in the media. Immediately after this, there was widespread and long-lasting speculation that the two of them were engaged in an incestuous relationship. For Angelina, who is extremely open about her sexuality, this was going too far. 'If I were doing that, I'd say it,' she countered. 'Everyone knows that about me.'

It didn't stop the rumour-mongering, and the continued coverage and conjecture deeply hurt both her and her brother. Years later, she still has to answer questions about that evening. 'I didn't snog my brother,' she explained recently. 'I wanted an Oscar my whole life – my father had had one. Me and my brother had a very difficult upbringing. We both survived a lot together and it meant a lot that he supported me my whole life. And in that moment, you reach to kiss somebody, and you end up kissing their mouth. Who cares? It wasn't like we had our mouths open, it wasn't some romantic kiss.' To begin with, the speculation was so intense that it seriously affected the family. 'I haven't talked to Jamie for a few months,' she told *Rolling Stone* in 2001. 'I think he – and I'm not sure – but somehow he made a decision to... to not be around me so much, so we wouldn't have to answer stupid questions.'

'We even talked about it: Do people actually really think that we're sleeping together? No – it can't possibly be. The Oscars, it was completely shocking to me that it was taken that way. I was hugging him, I kissed him.... If it seemed too long... He loves movies, my brother. He knows who won every Oscar. I was up for an Oscar. And he was so supportive. So when I said, "I'm so in love with my brother now," what I was trying to say was, more than getting a fucking award I can't believe how much this person loves me. And somehow that was turned into god only knows what. Basically they were completely missing the real story, which is how great it is that two siblings support each other – if you're in a divorced family sometimes kids get a lot closer and hold onto each other.'

'The world is a lot sicker than I thought,' she said to *The Mirror*, around the same time – a year after the incident. 'For some reason people thought it was more interesting to focus on something that was sick and disturbing rather than the fact that two siblings support and love each other. Unfortunately, it has put a distance between us, because Jamie now feels he has to keep a space between us.' Angie, who is invariably insouciant about what the press and public choose to believe about her,

The Beverley Hillbillies

was incensed and disgusted by the stories. In 2000, when she was promoting her next film, *Gone in 60 Seconds*, she used the publicity opportunity to hit back at one of the people who had made some of the cruellest jokes.

Jay Leno is the comedian host of *The Tonight Show*, NBC's well-known talk programme. He is famous for getting laughs at the expense of various celebrities (one of the most high-profile of which was Michael Jackson; as a witness in the abuse case, Leno was temporarily barred by the judge from making jokes about Jackson). Leno hadn't been pulling any punches with the Oscars material; on this occasion, he went too far, prompting Angie to directly attack him on camera.

Instead of talking about her new film, she handed him a transcript of the jokes that he'd recently used at her expense. 'I want you to read those out loud for my mother,' she told him. Leno, upstaged and humiliated on his own show, read out one or two before trying to excuse his behaviour as good-natured. It didn't wash. 'You make my mother sick,' Angie told him. She also made it clear what she and Billy Bob thought of *The Tonight Show*. 'We don't even watch your show,' she told him. 'We're doing more interesting things at home.'

COMMITTED RELATIONSHIP
Gone in 60 Seconds didn't get the expected plug, but Angie had showed herself more than capable of fighting her tormentors' battle on their own turf and terms. As it happened, the film didn't

need the extra advertising anyway. *Gone* was little more than a crowd-pleaser, but it grossed over $100 million at the box office in the US alone. Angie's bit-part as the girlfriend of a retired car thief (Nicholas Cage) was just what she needed, too – a break from the tougher roles she'd been working on for *Girl* and *Bone Collector*. It didn't require much more effort than looking great.

That wasn't all that was going on in her life. She had finally divorced Jonny after two years of separation, and – after a few false starts – had realised that things were getting serious with her *Pushing Tin* co-star, Billy Bob Thornton. Their relationship was already a hot topic in the media, partly because of their public displays of affection and unashamed confessions about their love life. 'When you're friends, and when you love somebody you tend to be as outspoken as possible, to make them feel good. You tell the world that they're wonderful, and you love them, and how great they are,' she explained.

Both had wanted to get married for a long time, but circumstances were difficult – not least because of Angie's recent divorce, Billy Bob's long-term partner Laura Dern (to whom it is rumoured he was engaged at the time), and their respective schedules and homes. Although it felt like it was Meant To Be, there would be plenty of complications on the way to the altar. One of her darkest (and most publicised) hours came only four days before their wedding.

On a handful of occasions, Angelina has spoken about the brief

The Beverley Hillbillies

time she was confined to a psychiatric hospital as a result of difficulties surrounding their relationship, just before they finally tied the knot.

Needless to say, speculation ran riot as to why she had been 'sectioned'. 'There are certain things that are true and not true about that,' Billy Bob confided to *US Weekly*. 'To put it in simple terms, we wanted to get married and we couldn't at the time. We soberly wanted to make sure feelings didn't get hurt. So we did wait, and it kind of made us both spin out a little. I was in Nashville, she was back in LA, and looming above us was the fact she had to leave for London soon.'

'We were becoming a family, and we had a family to think about: my family and his mother, his children, his ex-wife and everything. We wanted everybody's blessings,' Angelina remembers. 'What happened is we didn't know if we were going to be able to be together… I remember him driving somewhere and not knowing if he was OK. We had wanted to get married and then for all these different reasons we thought we couldn't.

'When I couldn't be near him, I started to go nuts. Then I couldn't find him. I thought I'd lost him. And I'm human. I felt lost and got sad to a point where I wasn't thinking clearly. If I'd been able to find him, I would've been fine. But I didn't want to hurt myself or anyone else. So I went into the hospital to make sure my blood pressure was normal and they ended up saying, "Maybe you should take a rest for a few days." And that was it. After a

Angelina Jolie

day or two, we found each other, and then I got better.'

Press speculation about the episode raged, with some alleging she had committed herself because she thought she had killed someone. 'Maybe part of me needed to shut down for a few days to process everything before. I don't know,' she said simply. One way or another, she found herself in a psychiatric ward – a situation that echoed her Oscar-winning role alongside Winona Ryder and that was not lost on the other patients.

'Some of them were aware of me, some of them had seen *Girl, Interrupted*,' she told *Rolling Stone*. 'I mean, to a lot of young girls, to all of us, there are these pictures in magazines of people that have their shit together where their lives are perfect. I think that somehow it was refreshing for these people that were struggling with the different things I've struggled with in my life to realize that it's not about... Certain things don't make it better, there isn't some other side of life, people aren't any different.'

Billy Bob's marriage to Angelina, shortly after she left UCLA, was his fifth. ('I've been married five times,' he said, 'and people think that's some bizarre thing. Yet I've got buddies who refuse to get married and have sex with 15 people a week. I'm like, "Which is better?" At least I was trying.') Once again, the fairytale wedding was shunned for a convenient and, above all, quick ceremony in Las Vegas. They tied the knot on May 5th, 2000, not long after the controversial Oscars ceremony. Laura, meanwhile, was oblivious to all this, only finding out about it when she read the

The Beverley Hillbillies

details in the press. 'I left our home to work on a movie, and while I was away my boyfriend got married and I've never heard from him again,' she told the *Daily Mail*.

'The wedding was perfect for us,' Billy Bob told *US Weekly*. 'It was cheesy and beautiful and profound and intense and light-hearted and humorous. It was everything.' Despite their A-List status, the cost of the wedding barely hit three figures. 'We were in a hotel bar,' Billy Bob described. 'I said, "I'll be right back." I asked a woman if there was any place to buy a ring. She pointed me to a jewellery store in the hotel lobby. But all the rings looked like something Zsa Zsa Gabor would wear. I found a woman outside with a jewellery cart and picked out a ring for 29 bucks. I'd never seen anything like it, and I've never seen anything like Angie. That's the idea, isn't it? Get something that has meaning.'

'It's sick how happy we are,' Angie admitted. 'You know, I used to hate people like us.' The marriage was certainly unconventional, but unconventional seemed to work for them. 'I'm so lucky,' she said about Billy Bob. 'It's beautiful. I am honoured to be with him. He's just an amazing person. He's an amazing lover and he knows my body. He knows things that I don't know. We didn't belong any place until we met each other. Together, we understand each other completely. We feel safe because we're so honest with each other. We don't worry about anything. We protect and care for each other. He knows how much I love him.'

Angelina Jolie

Musician Billy Bob even penned a song about their meeting, titled 'Angelina':

> I walked into an elevator
> And you walked into a wall
> You said you wanted to be with me
> But I never dreamed I'd have it all.
> They all said we'd never make it
> Two crazy panthers on the prowl
> They said we would only fake it for a while
> But we just looked at them and growled...

'We focus on each other in a way that's so intense that it's like that,' he told *Rolling Stone*. 'We also stalk each other around the house. In the kitchen. It's a constant dance, really, for us.' Whether they did fake it for the time it lasted, nobody knows except them; but one thing we do know is the lyrics of 'Angelina' were not Billy Bob's finest hour as a songwriter.

So began one of Hollywood's unlikeliest pairings. The press had a field day with their unexpected and eccentric marriage, and Billy Bob and Angie found themselves constantly in the limelight. Despite the intense misgivings of many close to them, for a long time things seemed to be working out between them. Both Angelina and Billy Bob were genuinely happy, and all too pleased to provide the media with tabloid-fodder both about their active and outré sex-life, and other unusual details of their relationship. One of the strangest of these was a fascination with blood

The Beverley Hillbillies

− a long-standing fixture for Angelina that began in her Goth-influenced teen days. She and her husband are widely known to have worn vials of each other's blood on silver chains around their necks.

'I've painted with it,' Angie admitted. 'There's something very primal and romantic about it. I've considered pouring it on my clothes but I think people might be a little upset about it. I'm trying not to upset people.' Also unorthodox was the choice of bedroom decoration − a framed message, 'To the end of time', written in her blood. 'If there were a safe way to drink his blood, I'd love to,' she once admitted. 'We've thought about it. You lay in bed and you just want to bite holes into each other. It's not about cutting yourself or some kind of weird thing − now it's just, "I want to eat him".' She is always keen when she makes slightly ambiguous remarks like this to convey that 'eat' also means fellatio. Angie gives good copy.

But she stressed that mutilation, occasionally a part of her earlier relationships, was now a thing of the past. 'It was a need, but I feel enough for my husband now that I don't have the need,' she said. 'In the past, I never met anybody that loved enough, that wanted enough, that was crazy or open enough.' She did still keep a knife (from an extensive collection of blades) next to the bed, but claims it was mostly used to open post.

The only other member of the family was Fat Harry the rat − Billy Bob had ignored the vet's pleas after the Vlad and Harry

Angelina Jolie

Dean Stanton episodes and given Harry to Angie as a wedding present. Harry – actually a female rat – lived in a cage near the end of their bed. He developed a partiality to pumpkin pie, which probably explains the name (Fat Harry's is a New Orleans burger restaurant). 'Billy found me one day sitting in the bathtub in my pajamas, the rat on my lap, feeding it pumpkin pie,' she admitted once. 'See, that's one of those things that only somebody that really loves me is going to think is cute.'

SUPERSTAR

With a new marriage, several new awards and a whole lot of media attention – not all of it bad – the future was looking bright. Angie's next project was unusual, but one that would take her career and profile to an entirely new level. *Tomb Raider* turned Angelina Jolie into an overnight sensation. But it also changed her in other ways, starting a whole new phase in her life and opening up doors she had never seen before.

The concept was odd in that *Tomb Raider* took its inspiration from a video game, rather than a book or theatre script. In the game, the extremely pneumatic British archaeologist Lara Croft athletically runs, leaps, shoots and fights her way around a series of 3-D mazes, solving puzzles and defending herself to get to the ultimate goal. Whilst the cutting-edge graphics and absorbing game-play attracted many fans, it is fair to say that Lara's 36DD pixelated chest did the same. Movie bosses realised that the appeal would carry across to the big screen: there was already a dedicated fan base, and it was the kind of film which would

The Beverley Hillbillies

make good use of the ever more popular special effects and CGI that were becoming inseparable from the blockbuster genre.

They also realised that Angie, with her stunning looks and previous portrayals of strong, uncompromising women, would be ideal for the part of a female Indiana Jones. 'It was obvious to me that Angelina was the only actress who could play Lara,' said director Simon West. 'We needed a stunning-looking woman but also a great actress who could pull such scenes off in a totally believable fashion. I thought only Angelina would be able to act her way out of tight dramatic corners while never losing Lara's sex appeal or winning qualities.'

Others – game fans, who take these matters very seriously, in particular – weren't so convinced. They weren't happy about an American being picked to play someone quintessentially British. Then there was the question of vital statistics: Angie, #1 Most Beautiful or not, didn't have the measurements of the original. 'I thought the breasts were even bigger than I had in the film,' she told the *Daily News*. 'I didn't think that was necessary, but obviously somebody disagreed. It's amazing how fascinated people are with breasts.' Given the game's demographic? Not really. She eventually came round to the idea and a compromise was brokered.

'She's Lara Croft, you know what I mean? It's a part of her character. I'll make it real simple for everybody. I'm a 36C. In the game, she's a DD. In the movie, she's a D. So we split the difference. Padded bras work wonders.'

Angie actually remembers playing the computer game when she was married to Jonny Lee Miller. Jonny was a fan and convinced her to give it a go. 'I tried, but I'd get frustrated,' she told *The Independent*. 'I could never get her over the wall, so I would just throw things.' Computer games are still predominantly a male pursuit – this one, particularly so. To begin with, she just wasn't interested. The game dealt with a fantasy world that she couldn't relate to, and there just wasn't enough of a hook to draw her in. That would all change when she learned a little more about what training for the role would entail: gymnastics, canoeing, kick boxing, weapons work, motorbike riding, yoga and husky dog racing, to name a few. Suddenly the prospect was looking a lot more interesting.

She spent three months in a tough training regime. 'It was just insane,' she told *What* magazine. 'But once I was skilled in everything, then it was just maintaining the strength to do it and the ability to every day have the same energy. I'm proud that I survived them.' She had to watch her diet, give up alcohol and cigarettes (she drew the line at coffee), and spend serious time in the gym to get into shape. As she went on, she began to see the appeal of her character. 'If Lara Croft has a problem, she gets up and fixes it,' she said. 'If she's frustrated, she breaks something.' Lara was an uncompromising character who takes problems in her stride. 'That's what life can be. I read something once: "What matters is how well you walk through the fire."

The Beverley Hillbillies

Those are the paths in life I like to take.' The film also brought her back together with Voight: in *Tomb Raider*, he plays Lara's own father.

In keeping with the attitude of her character, she insisted on doing most of the stunts herself. Immersing herself in the role in this way entailed a certain amount of danger, and she received many injuries in the six months of filming. Apart from the near-death experience when she was thrown from the husky sled, she picked up cuts, bruises, torn ligaments and burns. 'She was definitely thinking she was Lara Croft after a while,' said West, who found her enthusiasm increasingly worrying; he had to decide how much it was safe to let her get away with. 'She was totally fearless,' he remembers. 'I had to decide how much jeopardy I wanted to put her in and how much I wanted to beat her up.' He recalls one occasion when he had to draw the line. 'She was swinging on a moving log hanging 50 feet off a concrete floor and she wanted to take the safety harness off. If she fell, she would be dead. I didn't need that.'

The movie entailed spending six months filming in out-of-the-way locations such as Icelandic glaciers, the swamps of Cambodia, and even Windsor Great Park. World Rank Sleddog Racer JM, who worked with her in many of the stunt sequences, remembers how she never complained about the hardships. 'She just got on with it,' he says. 'She was a very together person.' This description is a far cry from the stories of the woman who was supposedly 'committed' to a mental hospital only weeks earlier.

Angelina Jolie

JM was particularly impressed with her generosity; at Christmas time, she bought the entire crew presents.

'She's a total individual,' he remembered. He has nothing but admiration for as an actress and a person. For six months he consulted, worked on the set and carried out the stunt work with her – only occasionally doubling for the few scenes that she didn't do herself. 'She was the easiest person to get on with,' he recalled in an interview with A Jot. 'Everyone liked her. And she got on really well with the dogs, too,' he adds. The sequences, which were filmed in the Pinewood Studios in Buckingham and in Iceland, required 60 husky dogs. 'And some of them really smelt bad.'

Now head of a top New Media Agency, JM has fond memories of the time he spent supervising Angie on *Tomb Raider*. His impressions belie some of the myths of the popular press, who frequently portray Angie as an eccentric personality with borderline mental health issues. In fact, 'she was one of the most grounded people I met,' says JM. 'She was a good laugh and she didn't have that **Prima Donna** attitude that some of the others did. She was just very down to earth.'

One of his favourite stories about her – and one of the most illuminating about her attitude – took place on the set at Pinewood. 'We were riding on the camera quad, with the dogs tied behind,' he recalls. 'We were going round the set, which was constructed a bit like a roller coaster – high-bank curves, chicanes and so

The Beverley Hillbillies

on. We took the corner at a...er, "reasonable" pace...and of course she flew off. She hit the wall, hard. She wasn't wearing much protective gear, no helmet or anything like that. She's lying there and I thought, "Fuck, I've killed the leading lady." I go over to her, and everyone's saying, "Fuck: what are we going to do if she's dead?" But she just dusted herself off and got up. She got loads of cuts and bruises in filming, but it just wasn't an issue to her. She was a consummate professional.'

Was that all? 'And she was one of the sexiest people I've ever met.' That's no surprise; Angie regularly hits the top of the Most Attractive lists. 'But she's not overtly sexy,' he stresses, against the received wisdom of carefully made-up and airbrushed model shoots (tattoos, rather than cellulite, being the major make-up issue). 'She's not that amazing-looking, but she's got a very attractive personality.'

The Hollywood publicity engine has the effect of pushing people into the boxes that the public want ticked; Angelina is not the kind of person that can easily be pushed, and there is evidently far more to know about her than is regularly featured in the magazines. 'There are people who want me to be a clean, simple package, and I don't understand that,' she says. 'I always thought that actors were supposed to be kind of crazy.'

Voight, too, praised her physicality, recalling how active and capable she was as a child. 'Angie was always very athletic. When I used to coach soccer, she was the best player on the team and the best at running in her class.' Angie remembers how her childhood influences had always tended in this direction. 'When I was a little girl I wanted to be Indiana Jones. I never think of women as not being strong.'

There was plenty in the Lara Croft that worked for her – which was just as well, as it has coloured the public's perception of her ever since. 'She's a bit like me," she told an interviewer. 'She is very feminine, very sensual, very loving, very emotional and a bit crazy – wild and strong.'

There is no question that Lara, like Angie, is an entirely self-sufficient person who does things on her own terms. One of the character's noteworthy points is that she does not have a love interest in the film. There are no displays of affection, however minor, but she is still an extremely sensual person.

'She has no sex and is never naked, but I think the fact she's a bit aggressive and free and wild makes her sexy,' claims Angie, whose thoughts on this aspect of her character's personality did not stop here. 'I could really imagine Lara not having a lot of time for men,' she told *Amica* magazine. 'Can you imagine that, Lara Croft as a lesbian? That would be a shock for the boys playing with their joysticks in their bedrooms around the world. At the end of the day I really like women. I'd love it if the girls in the cinema watching Lara Croft find me just as hot as their boyfriends do.'

The Beverley Hillbillies

Credit for all this goes to her new husband. 'I couldn't have played Lara Croft if I hadn't met Billy,' she told the *Daily News*. 'I wouldn't have had the confidence. Because, let's face it, it takes a lot of confidence to be this character. The adventure part of Lara Croft I could do. I'd be the first person to jump into a dangerous situation to try something. But it took Billy to make me feel very alive and very sexy. I mean, I feel sexier than I ever have in my life. I'm free, I'm in love, and I'm sexually satisfied.' Doubtless, Billy had sex like a true OCDer – by numbers.

The resulting film achieved exactly what it set out to do. The solid fan-base attracted millions of viewers, who were kept happy with a real-life version of their computer-game diva. *Tomb Raider*'s plot was unlikely, special effects and action sequences were heavily over-used, and the movie generally was more concerned to look good than deliver quality scripting or character development. Essentially, it was a vehicle for Angelina Jolie. Critics, whilst trying to hate it, nevertheless couldn't help but enjoy its inanity.

'*Tomb Raider* elevates goofiness to an art form. Here is a movie so monumentally silly, yet so wondrous to look at, that only a churl could find fault,' wrote Ebert. '*Tomb Raider* moves at a fast clip, and represents top notch eye candy. Of all this summer's mindless blockbusters, this is arguably the most fun... Regardless of its performance at the box office, *Tomb Raider* is a great way to cure the summer blahs, provided, as always with this kind of film, you short-circuit the thinking parts of your brain,' was Berardinelli's similarly grudging praise.

Angelina Jolie

The critics may have hedged their bets as to whether *Tomb* would score box office success, but West needn't have worried. It took over $130 million. Angie's own pay cheque was reported to be in the region of $7 million, but she wasn't quite prepared for the fame that this brought with it. Suddenly, she was every computer geek's idol. 'I didn't realise what I was getting into, really, before I took it on,' she admitted to *What* magazine. 'As the film went on, I started to realize the scale of it and her popularity and how much people knew her.'

She was also increasingly daunted by the scale of the marketing surrounding the production – even for her, it was unprecedented publicity. 'It's a bit strange and it's a bit daunting.' The fact was that *Tomb Raider* was set to define her as an actress for a long time. She had enjoyed making it and was pleased with the result, but knew that it wasn't perfect and that she could have done better (one of the reasons she agreed to the sequel two years later). 'I knew there would probably be some things in this movie that would embarrass me,' she said. 'I was expecting a lot of things just not to work or be too over the top. But, I ended up being happier than I thought I was going to be.' As the film was released and marketing hype reached a peak, she started to realise what this kind of fame could mean.

Surrounded by posters and merchandising featuring her own face – and body – she was shocked. 'I was trying really hard not to cry,' she told *Rolling Stone*. 'It was "Why has someone superimposed a gun right in between my legs?" or "My breasts

The Beverley Hillbillies

are big enough – why are they enhanced that much bigger?" I haven't adjusted my life that way,' she complained, realising the restrictions that this kind of fame could place on her freedom. 'It could fuck with your head.'

One thing it did do was bring her closer to her father. It was an opportunity to spend quality time with him, on and off the set, and to get to know him a bit better. 'We are great friends,' she said. 'We'd be friends if we weren't related. We can talk for hours.'

The Beverley Hillbillies

CHAPTER 5
A NEW ANGELINA

A NEW ERA

Tomb Raider was pivotal for Angie in many ways. Chief amongst these were the life-changing experiences she had whilst filming in Cambodia, picturesque and intriguing, but also famine-ridden and poverty-stricken after the bombing raids of Vietnam and then civil war. 'Cambodia is the most beautiful place I've ever been to,' she told *NYRock* webzine. 'I discovered things about what's happening in the world. Like my eyes started to open.' Up to this point, Angie'd had no experience of this world. She had enjoyed a relatively privileged and sheltered upbringing, even by Western standards. Cambodia was something completely different.

'I learned so much about these people and what they had been through. I expected to meet a certain kind of people because of that. And when I met them, they were so generous, spiritual, and open and kind.' Cambodia's bloody history has left many areas no-go zones, even years after the conflicts ended. 'I couldn't believe that they would have such patience with us, and such openness after all of that. There were areas we shot in, that we could only be in certain places, because they hadn't been de-mined yet...there are hospitals where kids are still being affected by stepping on landmines every day; it was horrifying and so sad. You never hear about that. To discover that kind of stuff was to really understand people in the rest of the world. So Cambodia was really eye opening for me.'

Angelina Jolie

Something about Cambodia touched Angie in a way she had never expected. It would turn out to be the beginning of a new chapter in her life, as – alongside her busy filming schedule – she immersed herself in charity work. She even went as far as to contact the United Nations High Commission for Refugees (UNHCR) in an effort to learn everything she could about the humanitarian crises going on around the globe.

'It was very clear to me there was a lot about this world that I didn't know,' she told the *Washington Post*. 'I felt really ashamed and ignorant. It just changed my life.' She spent much of the following year travelling to different locations around the world with the UN, flying to refugee camps and learning what she could about the situation on the ground.

Her first trip, at the beginning of 2001, was to war-torn Sierra Leone. She paid all of her own costs and did not insist on any special treatment, living in the same basic quarters and conditions that all of the volunteers did. 'I was shocked by what I saw,' she said in a subsequent press release. 'We cannot close ourselves off to information and ignore the fact that millions of people are out there suffering. I honestly want to help. I don't believe I feel differently from other people. I think we all want justice and equality, a chance for a life with meaning. All of us would like to believe that if we were in a bad situation someone would help us.'

All of this was in great contrast to her life as a multi-million

A New Angelina

dollar fee actress. She found that her experiences at the refugee camps threw her own problems into sharp relief. 'Celebrity is a weird thing,' she told *Nightline*. 'It can feel very empty at the end of the night to think, "Why is anybody giving any attention to me – because I made a film? Because I wore a dress to some event?" It's silly, and it feels very shallow because you're aware of how empty it can be. So, when you're doing something good, and you can bring attention to that or discuss that, then it feels like you have some sense in your life.'

It gave her a new appreciation for her own life, and a new sense of purpose. In the past, she told *APOnline*, 'I never had a sense of purpose, never felt useful as a person. I think a lot of people have that feeling – wanting to kill yourself or take drugs or numb yourself out because you can't shut it off or you just feel bad and you don't know what it's from.'

In the following months she took several trips, first returning to Cambodia. She then visited Pakistan. She was so moved by the plight of the Afghan refugees in camps there that she donated $1 million to the cause in response to a UNHCR appeal. In August 2001, the UN realised that her high-profile status and genuine enthusiasm could be put to good use, and she was given the honorary title of Goodwill Ambassador at the UNHCR's international headquarters in Geneva. 'We are very pleased that Ms. Jolie has generously agreed to give her time and energy to support UNHCR's work,' reported the UN High Commissioner for Refugees. 'She can help give a voice to refugees, many of

[below] Angelina Jolie's work at the UNHCR has taken her to Cambodia,
Chechnya, Tanzania, Haiti, Jordon...World Economic Forum at Davos.

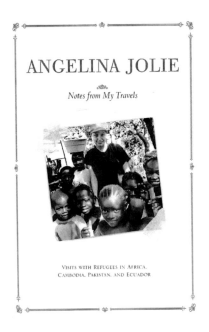

[top] The front and back covers of one Angelina's goodwill books, which help fund UNHCR

[bottom] A poster of Angelina's doodles while travelling for UNHCR

whom live in the shadows of forgotten tragedies. We are proud to welcome her to the UNHCR family.'

Tina Ghelli, public information officer for UNHCR, explained what her position would involve. 'Angelina is a Goodwill Ambassador for the UN's refugee agency. Her position entails travelling to countries that have refugees and aiding them by distributing food and supplies and making visits to schools and health centres. She makes about four or five of these trips a year and has been to places like Tanzania, Russia, Kosovo, Sri Lanka, Pakistan, Ecuador, and Sierra Leone.' Her movie-star status had the very welcome side-effect of raising the UN's profile amongst volunteers. 'Thanks to Angelina's involvement, UNHCR is now getting tons of inquiries from young people wanting to help the cause,' Ghelli said.

In fact, Angie had initially been sceptical about taking on this role. Her problem was not with the cause she would be representing, for which she had already proved she had the utmost respect and enthusiasm. She was more concerned that her portrayal as eccentric and unstable in the popular press might have a detrimental impact on the UN's work. 'I don't think you want me,' she told them. 'There are a lot of bad things written about me and my behavior. I could have a negative effect on your operations.' In the end, it was clear that the benefits would far outweigh any potential difficulties. At the end of her tour, she related how she felt about flying back to America. 'I felt sick because I started flicking through articles about parties, film

A New Angelina

ratings, who had this and who's the hottest that. I felt like I didn't want to return to that world,' she told the *Mail on Sunday*. 'You go to these places and you realise what life's really about and what people are really going through. These people are my heroes,' she said of the aid workers. Angie kept careful diaries during her travels, which have now been published as a book (*Notes from My Travels*, 2003).

The beginning of this new chapter in her life would also spell the end of an old one. For a while, things carried on relatively normally in her life. Aside from the trips to refugee camps she took with the UN, she kept up her filming schedule and spent time with Billy Bob. (One of the benefits to her charity work was that it diverted the press from the usual round of salacious gossip, giving them another side of her personality to write about.)

As 2001 rolled on, she began filming Life, *Or Something Like It*, in which she played a reporter who is told she has only a week left to live. May brought her first wedding anniversary, which she and Billy Bob spent in typical style. She flew out to meet him at Baton Rouge, Louisiana, where he was making his latest film. 'We got matching tattoos,' Angie said. 'We woke up, stayed in our pyjamas and went and got tattoos.' Her present to him also bordered on the macabre. 'I'd called his mother to find out where a lot of his family are buried and I reserved plots there so that one day, when we die, we'll be next to each other. That meant a lot to him.' Billy Bob's present to her was also unusual. 'He gave me a document witnessed by a lawyer that said he would be with me for ever. It's maybe a funny way of doing it, but we signed our life away to each other.'

Whilst all seemed to be going well with the couple, Angie's work with the UN had given her life a new dimension. Billy Bob didn't share her passion, and before long it would become clear that their interests were diverging. *Beyond Borders*, which she began filming at the end of that year, was another step along her road to self discovery. The film, a love story set against the backdrop of some of the world's worst humanitarian crises, brought together two of her passions, acting and charity work. The parallels with her own life were obvious, particularly given that many of the scenes were shot in places she was already familiar with, or would be soon – Chechnya, Cambodia, and Ethiopia.

For Angie, the romance that was a central part of the film was a necessary evil; it served the purpose of drawing in a wider audience in order to bring them the humanitarian message. 'It is a romance, yes,' she said, after critics aired misgivings about the plot. 'But it has been approved by the United Nations for the message it presents about the need in these countries. I'm so glad we got it near enough right to be approved by them. That was my goal. Of course the romance is there. It's just like if you tell people your article is about starving children, they won't read it. If you tell them I talked about sex, they'll read it.'

Due to problems with casting, finance and its uncomfortable

subject matter, the film had been a long time coming. Oliver Stone (of *Platoon* fame) was involved with it for five years, before Martin Campbell (*Goldeneye*) took over. The line-up of actors also changed repeatedly. 'When Angelina got involved, the way was cleared,' said Campbell. 'She's a very smart actress. Her instincts are good, and she uses them to make quick decisions on every scene. She moves very rapidly. After the "Lara Croft" adventure films, I think the public wants to see her act again. I mean, in a serious drama. She won an Academy Award and, since then, had chosen, mainly, commercial projects. Here, she returns to drama.'

Filming *Beyond Borders* only reinforced what Angie already felt, strengthening her desire to continue the charity work she had started after *Tomb Raider*. She had first read the script some years ago, but it took her recent experiences to realise the full impact of it. 'I'm sure all of us have had moments like that, like a book that did something to you,' she told *Star Interviews*. 'Or traveling somewhere and meeting that person. Whatever it is, it just does that. And you choose to take that different path in your life. But honestly, I didn't expect that when I read the script for *Beyond Borders*.

'I was moved by it, but I didn't understand why, or what that meant. And then I just found myself travelling, and in the middle of one of those countries. And I was completely changed. But I didn't handle it as well as my character did! I was a mess. People were surviving through amazing things, like losing their limbs to landmines. Or crossing borders with their kids. And they're smiling, and they're strong, and they're funny. You couldn't ask for better people to be around, and spend your time with.'

ANGIE'S MAD

Angie vividly remembers visiting an orphanage during her first trip to Cambodia, and the feeling of helplessness she took away from that. 'It was the moment,' she later told the *Virginian Pilot*. 'That moment. The moment in Cambodia when I held a starving baby in my arms. The first one I held. And, I...I didn't do anything. I didn't know that kind of suffering existed, at least not in a world that would be a part of me.'

The fact is, she was in an outstanding position to help, both financially and in her role as goodwill ambassador. But she felt she had more than that to offer. On returning to Cambodia, she arranged to adopt one of the orphans she found there whilst filming *Tomb Raider*. 'There are too many kids in this world who need a home,' she explained. 'I didn't want to be a mother just to see what I could create physically. I wanted to nurture and be a friend.'

'I was so taken with Cambodia and the nobility of its people,' she told the *Mail On Sunday*. 'I went back with the United Nations and that was when I decided to adopt a baby. I realised there was a lot I hadn't been exposed to in my life. I started to question a lot of things.' She described what it was like to become an instant mother, and the experience of finding her

A New Angelina

son. 'It's the weirdest thing to go to an orphanage and know that you are going to be bringing a kid home with you. He was the last child I met. He was asleep and wouldn't wake up, so at first I thought there was something wrong with him. They put him in my lap and I'd never held children so I was scared that he wouldn't be comfortable with me, but he just stared at me for the longest time and then we relaxed and smiled at each other. He accepted me at the same time that I accepted him. He opened his eyes and it was like he chose me. I like to think we chose each other.'

She adopted him on 10th March, 2002, giving him the name Maddox – Mad for short. Billy Bob took on joint responsibility as his adopted father, and his full name was Maddox Chivan Thornton Jolie. Unfortunately, what should have been a happy time was overshadowed by less pleasant events.

Angie's relationship with her father had, once again, become increasingly strained since the time they spent together on *Tomb Raider*. 'We seemed to understand each other and it was fun, but afterwards he returned quickly to old habits of being judgemental,' she told the *Radio Times*. Part of the problem was doubtless the unresolved issues she had always had about him walking out on the family when she was a baby. But there was more to it than those old tensions. His behaviour towards her had become harder and harder to tolerate. She remembers what happened when he took her to the airport before her UN mission to Cambodia. 'He gave me a letter in the car and said, "This is my truth, this is unchanging." I was unaware of what he'd written and said, "That's wonderful, I love you, see you later." Then I opened the letter. He'd written I was a bad person. I was upset and thought of a hundred replies, and then decided I don't value this person's opinion, so it's okay.'

Worse was to come when she adopted Maddox. She was keen to keep the news secret, but Voight instead announced it publicly. Angelina was incensed. 'I left him a strong message about how on the most beautiful day of my life, my first day with my son, he had cast this huge cloud. That day became about dealing with this thing that Jon had done.' After everything else that had happened, she was so angry that she asked Marcheline not to give him any more details about her life. She also promised herself that she would never speak to him again.

What made things harder still was her failing marriage to Billy Bob. Whereas they had initially been so happy together, the relationship rapidly deteriorated to the point where separation seemed inevitable. 'It seemed like we were passionately in love – and we were very much in love,' she explained to *The Mirror*. 'But it was a great, wonderful crush that came from fun and friendship. Then we started to do different things with our lives and halfway through our marriage we became very different people and we had nothing to talk about any more and we just had nothing in common.' There was widespread speculation that Billy Bob had not agreed with Angie's choice to adopt Maddox, and that this had brought things to crunch point. 'Our marriage

A New Angelina

was falling apart before I adopted and by the time Maddox came home, Billy and I were apart,' she claimed.

Both the public and their friends were surprised at how fast things went downhill. The best explanation seems to be that, whereas Angie changed very quickly, suddenly becoming more aware of herself and her priorities, the rest of the world stood still. Billy Bob got left behind. 'Suddenly I had a baby, and that child was the center of my life,' she said. 'Anything that took away from that or hurt that was going to have to go.' She recalls how Billy Bob didn't give her the support she had expected when she got involved with the UN. 'Why are you going to do these things? What do you think you can possibly accomplish?' he had asked her.

'I had to believe I could accomplish something. He also felt that I should focus more on our home, and I'm sure he was right in that. It takes a certain kind of husband to be fine with his wife focusing on something outward and not spending enough time on the home,' Angie explained. 'There wasn't enough respect coming from him and I couldn't put up with that any longer,' she later told the *Daily Mail*. 'I'm a very open and tolerant person, but there are certain things that I can't put up with and you have to draw the line somewhere. We became very different people – that can happen to anybody.'

'Life happens and there is a time when you are not going to be good for each other. It can be a very ugly, difficult time and during that time we just divided. We had nothing to say to each other. I had to survive and protect myself and he had to protect himself and do what he had to.' Angie filed for divorce in July 2002, after two years of brief but intense marriage. She also swore never to have a man's name tattooed on her body again; laser removal treatment was too time-consuming and painful.

Enlisting the insights of a relationship therapist, Rebecca Timlin-Scalera, *Cosmo* printed the following judgement. 'Angelina strikes me as someone who's passionate and focused. And when she commits to something, she commits one hundred percent, which is why she was so devoted to Billy Bob. The problem was that she and Billy Bob are both incredibly intense people, and it can be hard to sustain a relationship when both people are this over-the-top. They were so wrapped up in each other that it became difficult to strike a balance and devote energy to the other aspects of their lives, like their careers or a baby. People this passionate tend to fall out of love as intensely as they fall into it.' Even Angie had seen the danger of being so extreme. At the beginning of their marriage, she had remarked, 'We love each other obsessively, madly. It's all focused on each other, and we're going to explode.'

It was the fifth marriage that Thornton had seen end in divorce. When asked, he held up his hands and admitted that much of the fault was his. 'I am a scared person. I walked away,' he said. 'It's the most stupid thing I've ever done. I fell in love – the hardest I have ever fallen – and that was a scary thing. Nothing

A New Angelina

was her fault, absolutely nothing. It was all down to me.' The divorce itself would be finalised a year later, in May 2003.

Jon Voight had other ideas, and expressed them openly – much to Angie's disgust. As far as she was concerned, the final straw came at a time when she should have been able to count on Voight's support. Shortly after she separated from Thornton and filed for divorce in July 2002, Voight appeared on the *Access Hollywood* show. To begin with, he was dismissive of Billy Bob and Angie, and their chances of a successful marriage. 'I never had the feeling that they were going to make it, because of both of their serious problems...so I never really held out any hope.' He went on to suggest that she was mentally ill. 'Angelina has carried a lot of pain,' he said. Voight broke down in tears as he continued, 'I haven't come forward and addressed the serious mental problems she has spoken about so candidly to the press over the years, but I've tried behind the scenes in every way... They're very serious symptoms of real problems.'

Susan Margaret, who had witnessed Voight's infidelities and cult involvement, had the following to say to WENN. 'It makes me angry to hear Jon Voight saying on TV that Angelina has mental problems. Angelina is a healthy, wonderful person. She had a difficult time growing up with what was going on. She has a lot of hostility toward her dad. Knowing that makes you understand a little about some of the things Angelina has done.'

Aside from being highly disloyal, Angie was furious about what

[top] At the opening of *Tomb Raider* the strain of seeing their father with another woman is painfully visible on the faces of his children, especially James

[right] Marcheline Bertrand who acts as Angelina's agent but now suffers from uterine cancer

the accusations could have cost her. 'He had a lot of negative things to say, which shocked me and hurt me,' she said. 'Also, to do that considering I have a child... To try to hurt me, and to do it at a time – right at my divorce, as well – which, if I wasn't strong and focused, would probably have pushed me over the edge. This person could have had my child taken away from me. If this is taken seriously, that I am disturbed, what would that do to Maddox? Where would he go?'

Voight's behaviour, she suggested, was more consistent with his own 'serious mental problems', as he put it. 'I would love to have us all psychologically evaluated and let a court decide,' she said. 'If he was not a celebrity, everybody would think he was

A New Angelina

a crazy father of an actress, but he somehow has them saying, "We know this man, we've seen him in films, he can't be crazy."' Since then, she has remained estranged from Voight, even going out of her way to avoid him when their professional paths cross and they find themselves at the same events.

THE SINGLE LIFE
'I feel sexier out of my marriage,' Angie told *The Mirror*. 'I am much more sensual because I am not somebody else's wife.' Once the immediate shock and the media circus around the separation had worn off, she found she preferred it this way. 'I've found a new peace in my life,' she said. 'I don't think I'll ever get married again. I don't think I'm meant for marriage.' She had new priorities now. 'We're all meant to do different things and I've found that I love to travel, I love to feel useful and I want to learn about the world and do good things.'

Chief amongst these were her UN work and Maddox. Angie took to motherhood in a way that surprised those familiar with her wild-child past. As he grew up, conscious of his heritage and background, she also began to do more work in Cambodia. 'In my work, I get paid a ridiculous amount of money for what I do,' she confessed. 'I want always to give as much of it back to help these people. I have enough to take care of myself and Maddox, my child. That's all I need. But, of course, what I can give is nothing to what is needed.' It is her hope that Maddox will be able to serve his home country in some way in the future. 'He can be whatever he wants to be – and he will be,' she said. 'I

Angelina Jolie

am very focused on Cambodia. We have a project and there are hospitals, schools and an animal sanctuary named after him. He will have a very fortunate life and I want him to be responsible to his country, to know his language, his people, to do something to make it better for his people. If he, at 18, said, "I don't want to go there" I would have it out with him!'

Angie was so keen to involve her son in his home country that she built a house there – next to the $5 million wildlife refuge that she helped set up in northern Cambodia. Instead of being a western-style building with all the conveniences that might be expected of a Hollywood star, she kept it simple – 'three little wooden huts on stilts, with hammocks and a hole in the ground to poop in,' as she describes it. 'We're in the jungle. There are elephants and tigers.' Getting to the house was tricky, requiring plane, boat and car journeys (or, since she could afford it, one helicopter ride). Angie took flying lessons so that she would be able to take them in more easily in a light aircraft; when Maddox gets older, she hopes to spend quality time there with him. 'I promised him I would learn how to fly,' she said. 'You know, if you promise your kid something, you're stuck! So I got my pilot's license. I love flying. I've found that all the craziness in me now works perfectly under pressure in this environment.'

She hopes that Maddox will grow up speaking Khmer as well as English. 'They said to teach one language first. Khmer, the language of Cambodia, is very hard but I am trying to teach him some words.' This entailed learning it herself. 'I'm not very good

A New Angelina

at it – there are something like 27 vowels – and I'm frightened. But I will learn it,' she promised. Although she was keen for him to grow up with Cambodian influences and role models, it was not yet appropriate to move out to live there full-time. 'My son is still a toddler, and there are very real safety concerns – tigers and snakes, not to mention the 34 landmines that I've been told are still on my property – which mean we cannot live there permanently,' she said.

At least two of her many tattoos reference her son – in keeping with her tradition of marking significant milestones on her body. She had N11° 33' 00" E104° 51' 00" inked on her left forearm – over the lasered Billy Bob tattoo – representing the global coordinates at which she adopted Maddox. (Later, this would be supplemented by a second set, N09° 02' 00" E038° 45' 00", for her adopted daughter.) She also had a Buddhist prayer tattooed on her left shoulder, covering the Japanese symbol for death. The tattoo, written in Sanskrit, is a prayer for protection for Maddox. Although Angie is not a practising Buddhist herself, she wants her son to learn about it as part of his heritage.

TOMB RAIDER SEQUEL
Angie's next film role was a safe bet – a reprise of her hugely successful Lara Croft role. *Tomb Raider 2: The Cradle of Life* was her biggest movie to date. Her pay was reported to be $12 million – as far as director Jan de Bont was concerned, money well spent. 'There probably isn't another actress – or, indeed, actor – in the world who can accomplish the physical stunts

that Angelina can,' he said. 'She is fearless. She wanted to do everything herself. She is an amazing woman.'

Angie herself relished the challenge. 'Until the first *Tomb Raider*, I had not been very physical,' she said. 'I was athletic and tomboyish at school, but once you're out of school you don't tend to try new skills or do gymnastics. This film awakened the tomboy in me.' This time, the film chronicled Lara's search for Pandora's Box, an artefact with the power to destroy humanity. As before, it majored on special effects and outlandish stunts, strung together in long action sequences. 'The stunts were fun to do,' she told the *Sunday Mirror*. Cradle required her to learn a new set of skills. 'Horse riding was the most challenging. I had to ride side-saddle, but my horse hated the gunfire and was very skittish. The helicopter also scared him. I loved riding the jet-ski best; it was the first time I'd been on one.'

Despite immersing herself in the physical challenges that filming presented, this time Angie held back. Before, she would occasionally take unnecessary risks ('I'm an adrenaline-junkie, so I loved doing my own stunts... It has often verged on being suicidal'), which she saw as part of her overall self-destructive tendencies. This time she had new responsibilities. 'With Maddox in my life, I don't need all of that any more,' she said. 'He makes me feel deep, wonderful emotions. He makes me want to be alive.'

Maddox accompanied her wherever she was filming (largely England, but also Africa). 'He was only seven months old and

A New Angelina

With her mother,
Marcheline, Angelina
cradling Maddox soon after
she adopted him

there we were in the middle of Africa,' she said. 'I held him every moment the cameras weren't rolling. I lost count of the number of times he peed on my costumes. I got so little sleep some nights that I was exhausted, but it was such a wonderful feeling.'

Meanwhile, she was so taken with England that she bought a house there. After filming wrapped, instead of going back to LA, the two of them spent more time in Buckinghamshire. 'I feel so much more connected with the rest of the world when I'm there. I get access to what is going on globally. In America, you don't get enough news and information about the rest of the world.' The British media are also more forgiving than the American. 'Maddox and I can go out all the time. We choose to live a

Angelina Jolie

normal life and that's easier in England. When you don't put on the star attitude, you can live your own life.'

Living in England also gave her the opportunity to spend more time with her other ex-husband, Jonny Lee Miller. Following her divorce to Billy Bob, the pair were often seen together, sparking rumours that they would rekindle their romance. Jonny had recently broken up with his own fiancée, *Spooks and Holby City* actress Lisa Faulkner. However, both denied that there was anything more than friendship to their meetings. 'I talk to Angelina on a regular basis,' said Jonny. 'She's very well and quite sane,' he added in response to Voight's rumours.

'I'm sure I'll take a lover eventually,' Angie admitted. 'But at the moment I'm not seeing anybody. And I doubt I'll get married again. I am beginning to think I am really supposed to be alone, and that's OK.' The irony of playing screen-siren Lara Croft under these circumstances was not lost on her. 'But I find it really funny that I'm still seen as a sex symbol, considering I haven't had sex in a really long time.'

In the last *Tomb Raider* film, Billy Bob had been the inspiration for her confidence. This time, it was the only other man in her life: Maddox. 'Maddox and I are teaching each other about being mother and son,' she told *The People*. 'I don't have time for anything but casual friendships. Having Maddox in my life has made me a better person and I think it's made me a better actor. Everybody wants to feel useful. I was never fulfilled just as

A New Angelina

an actress. Being a mum's made an enormous difference to my life. I love being a mother.'

Rumour was that Billy Bob was still seeking a reconciliation, even at this stage, but Angie was adamant that it wasn't going to happen. 'Now I feel like I don't know him at all,' she said. 'We're not friends. We don't talk because I wouldn't know what to talk to him about.' When the divorce came through, she took full custody of Maddox. Nor would things get any better with Voight. 'I don't talk to my father now and it's a sad thing,' she told *The Mirror*. 'But what he did was unforgivable. He was very public about different things about me and said a lot of very harsh things. I think he's disappointed in me, but I need to stay very positive in my life, get as much accomplished, do as much good as I can and be a good parent. I don't want someone around who makes me feel bad, so I can't really afford to have a relationship with him,' she said, adding that Voight had completely misunderstood her. 'I have been crazy in my life, I have done wild things in my life, but I have never been a bad person.'

Angie's own family background, growing up with just her mother and brother after Voight walked out, convinced her that it was not important that Maddox had a father-figure – though it didn't make things easy. 'Without doubt, being a single mum is the hardest thing I've ever done,' she told the *Mail on Sunday*. 'My mum was a single mum but she was great. It is difficult, but it is 100 per cent more rewarding than anything else in the world.'

Angelina Jolie

Putting Maddox's priorities first meant that she had to make sacrifices; she realised that she could not date anyone she wanted. It would have to be someone who took fatherhood seriously, as she didn't want any more upheaval than she could help in her son's life. 'I don't feel like he is missing out. I feel a child should just be with someone who is totally committed to them. We live in a different world today.'

She was happy with her circumstances and, besides, didn't hold out much faith that the right man existed. 'That is where I belong and what feels really right to me,' she said. 'But finding the perfect partner who would just enhance all of that and not hinder it? I'm not counting on it. I'm able now to take care of myself and have confidence in myself and not look for protection and stability in another person.'

Despite the fact that she was a single mother, Angie was already putting thought towards adding to the family. 'I want to have a home that represents the world as I see it, with children from all different backgrounds, cultures and religions,' she said, suggesting a 'rainbow family' of 'enough for a small football team' (she has now scaled down her plans for a kind of United Nations orphanage – Brad Pitt is supportive but not unmindful of the adage that charity begins at home). She always saw adopting as the way forward, never seriously considering having a child of her own. 'I have always wanted to adopt. Having a child of my own would make me feel that there was a child out there who did not have a home because I had chosen to have a baby.'

A New Angelina

'I've watched Maddox playing with other children,' she said. 'I think having siblings will be great for him. If I were to have a child it would be one less child I was taking out of an orphanage – and that would haunt me.' Alongside her hopes to adopt again, she continued with the UN work and making significant donations of money to good causes. While she was filming *Cradle of Life* in Africa, she donated money to pay for a well. She also funded twelve school buildings in Cambodia, at the cost of £600,000. 'I make a ridiculous amount of money,' she admitted. 'Nobody needs that much to live on, and having all that money doesn't mean much if it's just sitting there. I put some aside for myself and my son, but with the rest I can build schools and do tangible things for other people.'

In fact, Angelina Jolie tops the do-gooders ratings: it is estimated that she gives a third of her income to charitable causes. Yet, she also gives time and often endures hardship to further the cause of UNHCR.

Angelina Jolie

UNHCR logo

CHAPTER 6
JOLIE FEVER

JOLIE FEVER

The rest of 2003 saw Angie work on a further five films, many of them concurrently. *The Fever* was a small production which opened the Virginia Film Festival. Starring Vanessa Redgrave as a woman coming to terms with her lifestyle in a war-torn country, Angie was one of a number of stars brought in for bit parts. Filming occurred in Wales, near Snowdonia, where she had also recently spent time working on *The Cradle of Life*. It was also the second time she had worked with Redgrave, who appeared with her in *Girl*.

Sky Captain and the World of Tomorrow was a much bigger production, and far stranger. This was another big-budget special effects bonanza. Set in a parallel 1939, when giant robots are attacking Manhattan, Angie played another minor part. This time she was Franky, an eye-patch wearing pilot who helps Jude Law (the eponymous Captain) and Gwyneth Paltrow save the world. *Sky Captain* was created almost entirely with blue-screen technology. Everything was shot in studio and all the natural effects were created by what are essentially special effects – CGI (computer generated imagery). According to no less a film guru than Steven Spielberg this is the future of film, which will include it going digital. Some of the critics compared *Sky Captain* rather to candy-floss: very pretty but syrupy and with little substance to stop it going quickly into the DVD market.

Angelina Jolie

Taking Lives, in which Angie played an FBI psychological profiler, was a little more substantial. Professionally, the role of Illeana Scott gave her more to get her teeth into. Meeting real profilers in the cause of research gave her an appreciation for the work, particularly the absorbing nature of the constant morbidity they work with. 'I've met a lot of them,' she told the *Cincinnati Post*. 'People who spend their lives focusing on things they have to take home with them and digest. It tends to affect their personal lives. I'm interested in those kinds of women.'

She found it intriguing that people could engage so thoroughly with such dark material, almost living it themselves in order to understand the personalities they are chasing. 'They're constantly digesting and analysing the dark side. So a lot of them aren't married or are divorced. Can't maintain relationships. My character's not socially connected to the real world.' There were elements of the existence she could sympathise with. 'I realised that I also observe and analyse human behaviour. That's what an actor does. So, there's an odd parallel.' No doubt it also appealed to the residual Gothic teen in her.

Maddox once again accompanied her on set, and she spent as much time as she could with him when she wasn't on camera. But the film, which features a number of brutal murders, was one she certainly wouldn't be letting him watch for a while. He was even disturbed by the publicity material he saw, which features her in the grip of a shadowy figure. 'He had a strange reaction when he saw it,' she said. 'He's used to seeing images of me.

Jolie Fever

But with this one, he realised that it was me and it looked like something was wrong.'

Taking Lives was criticised on the same grounds as her last serial-killer film, *The Bone Collector* (and, it seems, most serial-killer films since *Silence of the Lambs*) – it was clichéd. But her next film was something completely different from anything she had done before and, she hoped, more Maddox-friendly into the bargain. The animated comedy *Shark Tale* didn't even require her to act; it just put to use her signature husky voice as she played Lola, a seductive lion-fish/dragon-fish cross. The finished computer-generated character was, like all the fish, given the real-life actor's features. In Angie's case that included a prominent pair of lips. The good old DSLs.

Work on *Shark Tale* was a lot lower-key than some of her other projects, although creating a sexy fish was not without its challenges – for Angie as well as the animators. 'As Lola, I would think a lot of naughty thoughts and get into my kind of bedroom voice – my phone sex voice,' she said. Although, she added, 'If I was really a fish, a Japanese fighting fish would be my type.'

As hoped, Maddox appreciated her efforts this time. 'Maddox loves the movie, he was laughing at the première,' she told *The Mirror*. 'He was probably the best audience.' The concept of his mother acting a fish was a little too advanced to grapple with at his age, though. 'When I said "That's mommy," he just got really confused. I think he can understand seeing me in a film where

Angelina Jolie

it's actually me on screen. But the idea I entered the cartoon world and became a fish was just unbelievably strange to him and he's still trying to get over it.'

ANGELINA THE GREAT

Angie began work on her biggest film of the year in September. *Alexander* was a $150 million biopic about the life of Alexander the Great, the 4th century BC Greek king and skilled military tactician who took on and conquered the might of the Persian Empire. Directed by Oliver Stone, with whom she had narrowly missed working with on *Beyond Borders*, she would be working with many other stars – Colin Farrell, Anthony Hopkins, Val Kilmer and others. Angie's part was that of Olympias, mother of Alexander (Farrell) – despite the fact that she is only a year older than him.

Reactions to the film were mixed, and it courted controversy even before it was finished due to its depiction of sexuality in Ancient Greek culture. There are numerous sub-plots and suggestions involving homosexual relationships engaged in by key characters. A group of Greek lawyers initially threatened to sue Stone and Warner Bros. on the grounds that Alexander would be presented as bisexual.

Naturally, in our politically correct times homophobia itself could not be the reason for the outrage; the problem was that it was not a 'historically accurate' portrayal of the character. Stone counter-argued that the film was based on accurate historical sources and, after seeing an advanced screening, the lawyers relented...without, of course, really conceding.

Vindication, of a sort, came for the lawyers when the film was released. In the US, it failed to draw audiences and took only $34 million at the box office. The reasons were numerous, but looming large amongst them was the fact that American audiences just weren't happy with that kind of sexuality either. The Land of the Free couldn't get its head around the idea that Alexander might have swung both ways. 'There's a raging fundamentalism in morality in the United States,' Stone said at the UK première. 'From day one audiences didn't show up. They didn't even read the reviews in the south because the media was using the words: "Alex is Gay."'

'Kids weren't comfortable with men who hugged, a king who cries and expresses tenderness,' he told Variety. Stone also hit back at a population who could not understand a film unless it had a clear villain and simple plot; Alexander was too complex for 'conventional minds.' He was forced to make extensive cuts and changes for the DVD release. Overseas, where attention spans are longer and minds broader, *Alexander* was a success – earning a further $139 million and going to #1 on the charts in almost 40 countries. Critics, meanwhile, expressed dissatisfaction with the film's apparent lack of direction and clarity. Where they gave their approval, it was usually reserved for Angie, who capably managed to hold the screen and the audiences attention with her snake-draped portrayal of Olympias.

Angelina Jolie

As far as her own, off-screen sex-life was going, Angie was managing to court male attention almost as well as Alexander. On this occasion, she was linked to not just one but two of her co-stars – Irishman Colin Farrell and Jared Leto, who played Alex's very close friend Hephaistion.

Director Oliver Stone fuelled the rumours. 'Colin was all over her like a rash,' he told the *Sunday Mirror*. 'He was just falling in love with her, couldn't help himself. He was like a baby towards his mother. She was laughing at him. I don't know if actors sometimes act out their desires and he wanted to be the infant to her mother. It works.' Farrell didn't hide his feelings when asked, either. 'She's such a fucking brilliant actor, such a powerhouse, and she's such a sexy woman,' he enthused. 'It was amazing for me to look in her eyes and see the way she looked and held herself. She was so regal.'

Of course, after sexing her up to high heaven, he denied the rumours that he had been seen knocking on her hotel room door. In fact, the subject was mooted between them. 'Colin and I did become very close and the idea of dating one day was discussed,' Angie confessed. 'He is a very interesting man and artist. But we also talked about how we're maybe too similar. At this point, we're just the greatest of friends. I get linked with every co-star I ever work with and he's a great guy,' she said. 'But there was no affair. I had Maddox with me and he was always my priority. So, with the exception of a few nights when we'd all go out to dinner together, most of the time I was home with him. But,' she added cryptically, 'it's obvious Colin likes to work hard and play hard.'

She may not have been dating Farrell (or Leto, to whom she was also 'linked') at the time, but she had given up the celibacy that followed her break from Thornton and the adoption of her son. 'I went for about two years with no man around me, then decided to get closer to men who were already very close friends of mine. It's about all I can handle right now,' she told the *Sunday Mirror*. 'As crazy as that sounds, meeting a man in a hotel room for a few hours and not seeing that man again for a few months is about what I can handle. I've never had a one-night stand – these are people that I know very well. I can feel like a woman and get close to a man but it's not a relationship that interferes with my family.'

'I love getting to know them physically and mentally; they are not just random people I've met, they are these great people I want to be around for little bits of time,' she said. 'I guess what I'm saying is that they are these intimate friendships that are supportive about all aspects of me.' That is as far as it went. Intimacy, as always, was very much on her terms. 'I do get a message every once in a while if they've seen me on C-SPAN!' she admits.

As far as a long-term relationship went, she wasn't ruling it out any more. But again, it would have to be the right person, and it would have to be on her terms. 'Somebody said to me – we were talking about relationships and I agreed with them – they felt you have to find a person that you share the same values with and the same way of approaching life and family. That takes a lot,' she said. 'I'm just still coming to terms with exactly what that is for me, but I would be looking for the best father in the world and a guy who is up at night trying to figure out how best to do some good things, things for other people. Until then I'll just stay where I am.' But not for too much longer.

Jolie Fever

CHAPTER 7
HAPPY ENDINGS

HAPPY ENDINGS?

'I did not shag Brad Pitt. No, absolutely not.' Angie was typically forth-coming when a tabloid reporter tried to interrogate her on the low down about her supposed relationship with the Hollywood heart-throb. The rumours would turn out to be the best-known celeb story in history, providing journalists with more column inches than they knew what to do with.

It all began during work on *Mr. & Mrs. Smith*, the biggest film that Angie had worked on to date. 'Happy endings are for stories that haven't finished yet' was an appropriate tag line, given the ongoing situation that resulted. The suitably unlikely premise for the movie centres around a couple who, dissatisfied with their marriage, suddenly discover that they are both trained assassins hired to kill each other. Brad and Angie's fee for *Smith* was $20 million, which put her amongst only a tiny handful of highest-earning female actresses – perhaps only two or three others, including Julia Roberts.

When filming started, Brad was still together with *Friends* star Jennifer Aniston, whom he had married in July 2000 in a $1 million ceremony. The couple originally met on a blind date set up by their agent. The couple had always been in the public eye, eagerly tracked by the paparazzi wherever they went. Soon, that attention would be turned to a third party.

Angelina Jolie

Brad has frequently been named 'sexiest man in the world' and other similar accolades. Perhaps Jennifer understood the risks of putting the world's sexiest man in the same room as the world's most beautiful woman. Much of the previous year had seen them filming in different locations, sometimes going weeks or months without seeing each other. Clearly Jennifer was worried; she insisted on being present when *Smith*'s sex scenes were filmed between Brad and Angie.

Truth be told, things hadn't exactly been rosy for Hollywood's golden couple, Brad and Jen. Their schedules had long been a cause of tension and, adding to the problems, were said to be their differences over whether to start a family. The widespread rumour was that Brad wanted children, whereas Jennifer didn't want to take the time out of her filming schedule and put her body through the strain of childbirth, knowing it would take a long time to get her career back on track. In an interview with *Hollywood Rag*, she was quick to deny this. 'A man divorcing would never be accused of choosing career over children,' she said. 'That really pissed me off. I've never in my life said I didn't want to have children. I did and I do and I will! The women that inspire me are the ones who have careers and children; why would I want to limit myself? I've always wanted to have children, and I would never give up that experience for a career. I want to have it all.'

Whatever the back story, the tabloids immediately seized on Brad and Angie's time filming *Smith* as the reason for the break-up

Happy Endings?

of Hollywood's most publicised marriage. Angie, with two failed marriages and a sex, drugs and wild-child past, was naturally cast as the villain of the piece. And, of course, it is true that she did become close to Brad during filming. 'Yeah, they have gotten close because they've been working together, but that's it,' said Cindy Guagenti, Brad's agent. But asked whether their on-screen chemistry ever crossed the line into off-screen adultery, Angie is absolutely clear: 'To be intimate with a married man, when my own father cheated on my mother, is not something I could forgive. I could not, could not, look at myself in the morning if I did that.'

It didn't matter. As far as the media was concerned, a vixen with a reputation for sexual shenanigans was a far better reason for Brad and Jen's split than the 'irreconcilable differences' cited in the divorce; Jen filed in March 2005, two months after they separated. They had made an 11th hour effort to patch things up with a Christmas holiday to Anguilla in the Caribbean, though many suggested this was little more than a publicity stunt intended to offer the paparazzi plenty of 'happy family' shots.

The story goes that Brad put the romantic break on hold to fly back to the US for a day in order to watch a football game; that, it appears, was the final straw. The announcement was accompanied by statements that it was 'the result of much thoughtful consideration,' and 'nothing to do with recent tabloid speculation.' They were 'committed and caring friends with great love and admiration for one another.'

Angelina Jolie

The media feeding frenzy surrounding the so-called Pitt-Jolie-Aniston love triangle was outstanding publicity for *Mr. & Mrs. Smith*. Brad and Angie both already had enormous fan-bases, and this only raised their profile further. 'This is like hitting the jackpot,' one movie advertiser claimed. At the beginning of the year, *Smith* was billed as another run-of-the-mill summer action film, likely to play second fiddle to blockbusters such as *War of the Worlds* and *Fantastic Four*. With the announcement about Jen and Brad's separation in January 2005, suddenly everybody knew about *Smith* too. The film went on to take $50 million at the US box office in its opening weekend.

One of the most painful aspects of the separation for Jennifer was this relentless commercialisation of her failed relationship. 'It's been very important for me not to read anything, not to see anything,' she told *Vanity Fair*. 'It's been my saving grace. That stuff is just toxic for me right now. I probably avoided a lot of suffering by not engaging in it, not reading, not watching.' What really rankled was that, as the 'abandoned woman', she was immediately cast as the victim. Sympathy and its attendant condescension were all that she could expect. 'I've worked with this therapist for a long time, and her major focus is that you get one day of being a victim – and that's it,' Aniston continued. 'Then we take responsibility for our own input. To live in a victim place is pointing a finger at someone else, as if you have no control. Relationships are two people; everyone is accountable. A lot goes into a relationship coming together, and a lot goes into a relationship falling apart. She'd say, "Even if it's 98 percent

Happy Endings?

the other person's fault, it's two percent yours, and that's what we're going to focus on." You can only clean up your side of the street.'

Brad and Angie – dubbed 'Brangelina' by the press, as Affleck and Lopez had been dubbed 'Bennifer' in the previous year's celebrity love scandal – maintained, throughout filming *Smith* and for months afterwards, that they were 'just friends'. Tabloids and magazines had other ideas. Angie became the subject of hundreds of uncharitable headlines: 'Aniston and Pitt latest in long line of prey devoured by Jolie.' 'Angelina, man-eater, makes short work of unwary husbands.' 'Angelina has a mouth designed for Hoovering up husbands,' and many others. A few of the more perceptive articles stepped outside the media circus ring and suggested that the cause for Jen's unhappiness might be something else – Brad's insensitivity, for example. Even during their 5-year marriage, Brad was famous for his bacheloresque ways. His image was one of a motorbike-riding party-animal, more concerned with looking good than doing good, who could often be seen smoking the evening away and playing pool with his filming buddies – though this, too, was all about to change.

'I don't think he started an affair physically, but I think he was attracted to her,' was the assessment of Courtney Cox, Jen's *Friends* co-star. 'There was a connection, and he was honest about that with Jen. Most of the time, when people are attracted to other people, they don't tell. At least he was honest about it. It was an attraction that he fought for a period of time.' The occasional minority report made no difference and, ever since, Angie has been 'the woman who broke up Brad and Jen'. Whilst there is now no question that he and Angie are romantically involved, they were careful to keep their relationship under wraps for a long time – even after the separation. For months, they maintained that they were 'just friends', despite the fact that they were frequently seen out and about, and often flew to far-flung parts of the world together. 'People want an answer about what's happening in my life and my family, but I need to know what's happening first,' Angie offered. 'And I don't plan to discuss it before then. It's not about censoring myself. It's that there's nothing to say until I know that there's something to say.' But it seemed that the cover of 'travelling companions' couldn't last for ever.

On an almost daily basis, new photos appeared of the two together. Although these were often chance pap shots, or pictures for further *Smith* publicity, it wasn't restricted to that. In July 2005, *W* magazine published a 60-page spread entitled 'Domestic Bliss.' The concept had been conceived by Brad himself, and featured him and Angie in a 1963-style home-maker setting surrounded by blond 'Bradlet' children.

This was one occasion where Jennifer Aniston felt she had good cause to be outraged. 'You want to shake the shit out of him and say, "Your timing sucks!"' *Vanity Fair* quoted one of her friends. 'He's made some choices that have been tremendously insensitive.'

Happy Endings?

'Is it odd timing?' Jennifer asked herself. 'Yeah. But it's not my life. He makes his choices. He can do whatever. We're divorced, and you can see why.' Jen has famously suggested that Brad always did lack a certain empathy. 'I can also imagine Brad having absolutely no clue why people would be appalled by it,' she adds. 'Brad is not mean-spirited; he would never intentionally try to rub something in my face. In hindsight, I can see him going, "Oh – I can see that that was inconsiderate." But I know Brad. Brad would say, "That's art!" There's a sensitivity chip that's missing.'

Brad's crime does seem to have been insensitivity, rather than anything malicious. On other occasions, he has ardently defended Jen against the increasingly hostile attitude of the press. 'These guys have been incredibly despicable this round,' he said. 'They should literally be hung up and flogged. You wouldn't believe the shit they've been saying to Jen. She doesn't have a nasty bone in her body, and they are yelling horrible things to get a rise out of her so they can get more money for their pictures.'

As time went on, it became obvious to all that Brad and Angie were an item – despite their continued denials. The only question left is when they finally got together. Whilst this can only remain in the realm of speculation, the extremely unfashionable idea that it occurred after Brad and Jen's separation does seem likely, whatever attraction was present beforehand. In June 2005, Angie summed up the situation herself in an interview with NBC's *Today*. 'I wouldn't be attracted to a man who would cheat on his wife,' she said. Of course, she was well aware that, whatever the truth, nothing she could say would make the blindest bit of difference. 'You and I both know I could make a thousand statements right now and it doesn't matter.'

BRANGELINA

Once again finding herself one half of a celebrity couple, Angie started to put down roots with Brad. To begin with, things were low-key, in keeping with their reticence about the relationship. As time went on, their denials took on the character of a self-deprecating charade, almost a joke on the media that so badly wanted them to admit the obvious.

In April 2005, they were snapped on holiday on a Kenya beach (at least, by some paparazzi. *Star* magazine made do with pictures of the couple walking on different beaches, clumsily edited together). 'You've got to be kidding me,' Brad is reported to have said when he saw the pictures. 'Is there no deserted beach anywhere on this planet?' The plot thickened when stories broke that armed security guards had rushed to Angie's £1,200 per night hotel suite when other guests raised the alarm. For a moment, it seemed likely that a wounded animal had broken in, or that the pair were being attacked. The guards retreated sheepishly when it transpired that the noise was due to 'intense lovemaking.'

Brad and Angie could often be seen in less exotic circumstances. He was frequently a visitor at the home in the Buckinghamshire

Happy Endings?

village that she had bought whilst filming *Tomb Raider* at the nearby Pinewood Studios. Locals often saw them drinking together at the pub or shopping in Sainsbury's. Brad even used to pick up her son from nursery school. 'Brad would come down by himself to pick up Maddox,' one pre-schooler's mother told the *Daily Mail*. 'He seemed very pleasant, if a bit shy, and would just hang around waiting with the other parents. It was surprising how quickly a lot of the mums, who normally send their nannies down to collect their kids, started picking them up in person.' Things were changing fast for Brad, and his partying days seemed to be receding into the past as he took on new responsibilities: whereas his friends had speculated that Angie, with her eccentric past, might be a bad influence on him, exactly the opposite seemed to be the case.

ZAHARA

3 years after Angie adopted Maddox, there was a new addition to the family. This time, the adopted child was a daughter, an AIDS orphan from Ethiopia. Brad accompanied her to Africa, despite the fact that he was recovering from viral meningitis. Zahara (a name which means 'flower' in Swahili) had been born on January 8th, 2005. Her mother had died of AIDS, initially a real worry. 'There was a fear that she had HIV,' Angie said in interview on CNN. 'And the upsetting thing was that I was sat down and it was explained to me that – that, don't worry, because, in this country, it's not a death sentence.' Much to her relief, Zahara tested negative anyway. Angie told how Maddox's wishes had been instrumental in choosing his sister. 'My son is in love with

Angelina Jolie

Africa, so he has been asking for an African brother or sister,' she told The Daily Mail. The adoption went ahead on July 6th. Her new daughter's full name was given as Zahara Marley Jolie – the middle name being a reference to the Jamaican Reggae singer.

The family returned to the United States, but almost immediately Zahara became ill and was taken into hospital. She was diagnosed with Salmonella and, for a while, seemed close to death. 'She was six months and not nine pounds,' said Angie. 'Her skin – you could squeeze it and it would stick together.' Fortunately, Zahara quickly recovered; one of her nicknames is now 'Chubby'.

Although Angie was happy with her new family, there was still no evidence of a reconciliation with her father. In fact, Voight made things somewhat worse after he appeared on TV wishing his daughter, grandson and new granddaughter well. At the British Academy of Film and Television Arts Tea Party, he gave the following message: 'Maddox just had a birthday. Happy birthday, Maddox! Five years old – it's a big one! You're going to be a young man, and I send my love out to you. And send my love to... uh...Shakira...and Shahira... Is it Shakira or Shahira?' he finally asked the reporter.

Around the same time, speculation became rife that Angie was pregnant. Naturally, she and Brad didn't give anything away themselves. During filming of The Good Shepherd with Matt Damon and Robert de Niro, which started shooting in August,

Happy Endings?

it was reported that significant alterations had to be made to her costumes to give her more room. She is also said to have cancelled a day's filming due to morning sickness.

Meanwhile, Brad and Angie finally went public about their relationship. In December, they announced that Brad was also going to become Maddox and Zahara's adoptive father, leaving no room whatsoever for the public to think they were anything other than a family. Part of the adoption process was the legal requirement that the proposed name-changes of the children to Jolie-Pitt be advertised in the local newspaper. The bid was approved in January 2006, finally putting an end to months of speculation. Also beyond doubt was Angie's growing bump, and January saw her confirm that she was pregnant with Brad's baby, due in May. Forced to find new rumours, tabloids immediately suggested that a third marriage was only weeks away. 'They want to get married as soon as possible,' reported *The Mirror*. 'Her pregnancy made her realise she wanted to be married. There'll be very few people – maybe only four guests.' Reports that Brad had been seen shopping for an engagement ring have so far come to nothing. *Esquire* magazine reported that Brad, a supporter of gay marriage, has instead suggested they would tie the knot only when same-sex couples were legally permitted to do the same.

Angie's influence on Brad has undoubtedly been a positive one. Accompanying her on some of her many charity trips, he has developed his own philanthropic tendencies and taken an apparently genuine interest in the humanitarian missions and situations he witnessed. His sudden transformation astounded Hollywood, who never saw him as a campaigner for justice or famine relief. He has become involved in a number of high-profile projects, including AIDS research and the ecologically friendly rebuilding of New Orleans after the destruction left by Hurricane Katrina. Brad is a keen amateur architect – something that drove Jennifer Aniston to distraction, as his determination to oversee the rebuilding of their house stretched the project out over two years. Perhaps most significantly, he was encouraged by Bono to take part in *Live 8* and raise support and awareness for Africa. He is also a celebrity promoter and spokesman for the Make Poverty History campaign.

SHILOH

In a bid to escape from the inevitable media circus that would surround the birth of their child, Brad and Angie made the extreme step of flying out to Namibia. Angie had fallen in love with the country after visiting during the course of filming *Beyond Borders*. Aside from the obvious advantages of privacy, part of the decision was based in a desire to contribute to the country's healthcare. Their donation of $300,000 was welcomed by the African country's hospitals, as were the further pledges for schools and a community centre.

The couple spent the two months before the birth at a beach resort in Namibia, in an attempt to seclude themselves from any intrusive paparazzi who might have tried to follow them. Officials

Happy Endings?

made sure that they were screened off and security were placed around the hotel. Police even arrested some photographers and confiscated film. All of this was a small price to pay; it was hoped that the celebrity pair might bring some lasting benefit to the country's economy. 'We are honoured they chose Namibia,' said local governor Samual Nuuyoma. 'This family has opened the doors for us to the world.'

The baby was born on May 27th. The labour was comparatively brief, as it was a breech delivery and it quickly became clear that a Caesarean would be required. Brad was on hand to cut the umbilical cord himself. They named the new daughter Shiloh Nouvel Jolie-Pitt. The name Shiloh is of Hebrew origin and means 'sent', a figurative term for the Messiah. It can also mean 'peaceful'. Shiloh was offered Namibian citizenship by the government.

Rather than entrust the first snaps of their new baby to paparazzi, Brad and Angie decided to put the opportunity to better use. Initially, they kept up a strict policy of silence. 'Any information relating to the birth of the baby will be made available to the public soon,' Nuuyoma announced, shortly after the birth. Celebrity baby photos are very big business, and prices can run into the millions of dollars. Rather than give that away to the paparazzi who had tormented them for so long, the couple turned the situation around to their own benefit. 'While we celebrate the joy of the birth of our daughter, we recognise that two million babies born every year in the developing world die on the first day of their lives,' they reported on *E! Online*. 'These children can be saved, but only if governments around the world make it a priority.' They arranged to sell the first pictures of Shiloh themselves after a private photo shoot, giving the substantial proceeds to charities supporting African children. Reuters reported, 'The photos, which are expected to fetch millions of dollars, will be licensed to media worldwide by Getty Images, which said it will make no profit from distribution of the pictures of the Hollywood couple's baby.' *Hello!* gained the British rights for $3.5 million, whereas in the States, *People* magazine forked out $4.1 million.

WHAT THE FUTURE HOLDS

'Who wouldn't fall in love with Brad?' Angie recently said to The Mirror. The paper was keen to know about their future plans, but typically gained little of concrete use. What does seem clear is that the couple is working to create solid foundations for their relationship and family. 'Above all else, we're very good friends, we respect each other, we confide in each other and we have a great time together,' she said. 'What may happen from now on is something even we can't begin to guess at.'

In the face of continued speculation about the state of their relationship and possible marriage, they remain as detached and uninterested as ever. 'If we were to worry about what's been said over the last few months, we'd never have enough time for the really important things in life,' Angie said. 'Neither of us has ever spent time bragging about our private lives, or confirming or denying rumours. We're too old for that. If there are people out

Happy Endings?

there who want to live from speculation, let them. But they can't count on us to fuel that game.'

Jenny Shimizu has had one or two thoughts in that direction though. Since Brad Pitt came onto the scene in 2005, Jenny has gone so far as to express doubts about showbiz's hottest couple, suggesting that he would never be able to satisfy Angie's Wanderlust. 'Maybe she would settle down and be with one person but I think she goes looking for excitement all the time,' she told *The Sun*. 'Her passion is people and it's hard to just settle down with one person when you have a whole world in front of you. I'm not saying she sleeps with a lot of people. But I can't imagine her just being married and being happy.' Brad, by contrast, is the stay-at-home type. 'It seems like he comes from a different place. He wants to have kids and he wants to have a perfect marriage. She's a tough woman who will do everything she wants to. I don't think there is any way of controlling Angelina. She's not going to be a housewife.'

One of the things Angie has talked about, in interview with CNN back in June 2006, is the couple's intention to adopt another child. 'Yeah, next we'll adopt,' she said, although deciding from where wasn't so easy. 'We don't know which country. But we're looking at different countries. It's going to be the balance of what would be the best for Mad and for Z right now. Another boy, another girl, which country, which race would fit best with the kids.' There was even the possibility that the child would come from the US, a Hurricane Katrina orphan.

Angelina Jolie

Other than that, it seems that Angie's film career is showing no signs of slowing down, with half-a-dozen films planned or in production. After *The Good Shepherd*, a thriller about the early years of the CIA, comes *Beowulf*, an adaptation of the epic Old English poem. Amongst her future projects is the possibility of a leading role in *Sin City 2.*

Happy Endings?

CONCLUSION

CONCLUSION

One of Hollywood's wildest children has mellowed in recent years. From her early beginnings as a drug-taking, knife-wielding punk, she has developed first into a stunning model and then used her looks and talent to build a career as a successful actress. After that she has put her fame to work in helping the world's most underprivileged people. There is in many of the superstars who do similar work more than a taint of them being more interested in leveraging their compassion portfolio than assisting the causes they support. Charity, after all, is now another global industry for branding the image. Nevertheless, it is as an actress on which Angelina's fame rests.

Jeff Blayblock-Rayner, a celebrity photographer from Angie's home town of LA, tries to sum up her charm. 'Yeah, she's got something special. She has a natural hold over her own appearance. She is genuinely beautiful. It's a natural beauty. A lot of today's celebrities spend three hours in make-up before they come out looking shiny, and anyone can do that. I've seen Jolie with no make-up on and she is still stunning. It's extremely unusual. She carries herself well. She's not one of these divas who comes across as demanding everything all the time... She seems down to earth, and all the more beautiful because of it.'

Mark Bennett, casting director for *Alexander*, supports this; part of Angie's appeal is her unprepossessing charm. 'In this time in which celebrities go out of their way to show how "normal" they are, how "just like us,"' he says, 'Angelina Jolie makes no pretence of the kind. Her life is writ large, and unabashedly in the public eye. She doesn't want to be like us. As such, we find ourselves wanting to be like her. Also, in a time when ingénues are rewarded for cuteness and a certain dewy sexlessness, Angelina projects the most modern of sexualities: carnivorous, omnivorous, and unapologetic. Most Hollywood actresses cast themselves as the girl next door; Angelina Jolie doesn't look like she's ever lived next door to anyone.'

But there is now far more to her appeal than mere good looks – which, she would be the first to say, are hardly the limit of her persona. She has put her wealth, talent and influence to good use, showing a side of herself that most people never expected even existed. Although she still thinks of herself, at heart, as 'just a punk kid with tattoos', she has broken out of the mould and undertaken a programme of charity work amongst the poor and underprivileged – concerns that most people in her line of work know nothing about, and have no wish to know about.

'I hope it has brought more awareness,' she said of her role with the UN. 'That's all I can hope for. I know what it's done for me, but I hope it has brought more awareness. I feel it has because people tend to ask me questions, and I have received a lot of letters from young people talking about the things they are doing to make a difference... The most important thing, or the thing I

Conclusion

think I accomplished most was going to these places and sitting down with the families for about an hour. What matters most of all is that you go out of your way to sit down with people and listen to their stories and talk with them and show them somebody cares and is listening.'

More recently, Angie has become involved in political lobbying. 'In my early 20s I was fighting with myself,' she says, referencing her less altruistic past. 'Now I take that punk in me to Washington, and I fight for something important.' Of particular concern is the issue of children's rights. At the World Economic Forum in Switzerland, she slammed the Bush administration for refusing to sign a UN bill of rights for children. She has also pushed three bills to protect children, working with Hillary Clinton to approve billions of dollars worth of funding for education in the poorest areas. 'The more children I have, the more I feel it's my duty,' she said. Her adopted family is just one facet of this activity; whilst the long-term and large-scale plans play out, she feels she can make a difference on an individual level too.

Naturally, her charity work has its sceptics, particularly in the light of the constant tabloid rumours about other aspects of her personal life. But Angie has gradually come to find that less troubling. 'I don't care what people say,' she told the *Sunday Mirror*. I feel I'm doing some good and that's what's important.' This desire to detach herself from celebrity culture – except where it can be exploited to good use, as in the case of the photos of her newborn daughter – is one of the main reasons she decided to move to the UK. 'I didn't move to England for the weather,' she claims. 'But the quality of life is better and I have a lot of friends there. It's hard to feel healthy in LA because you can't drive down the street without seeing which movie is opening.'

Broadening her interests and looking outside of herself has led to a more centred, peaceful existence for Angie. Although she is highly involved with her family and charity work, she is keen to continue making films as well. 'In the past, I needed it because I was living vicariously through the characters I played,' she said. 'I'm able to love acting now.'

Regardless of the media's continual speculation, it is abundantly clear that there are four mainstays to Angie's life: her films, her children, her husband in all but ceremony and her charity work. These are her passions and, whatever else the future brings, it seems fair to say that more of each of these will feature heavily.

Conclusion

I don't believe in guilt, I believe in living on impulse as long as you never intentionally hurt another person, and don't judge people in your life. I think you should live completely free.

Angelina Jolie

We come to love
not by finding the
perfect person,
but by learning to
see an imperfect
person perfectly.

Angelina Jolie

1988 Oscars Award Ceremony: Jon Voight with Angelina and James. His 13-year-old daughter still has braces on her teeth. Both children are slightly self-conscious about the absence of their mother.
Voight had not been nominated but he watched his friend Dustin Hoffman take Best Actor for wiping Tom Cruise off the screen in *Rain Man*.

Angelina Jolie and her mother, Marcheline Bertrand, at the after-party of the premiere in Los Angeles of *Original Sin* on 31 JUL 2001

Charbonneau/BEI / REX FEATURES

Angelina and her brother James at
the premiere in New York of *The Bone
Collector*: October 1999

Erik Penzich/ REX FEATURES

At the 1998 BAFTA Film Awards
ceremony in London, Angelina Jolie
and her first husband, English actor
Jonny Lee Miller.
Richard Young/ REX FEATURES

Angelina, in Novemeber 2004, on the German TV show *Wetten Dass*, letting a boa constrictor curl around her. She loves snakes. Jonny Miller had to share their bed with her pet albino corn snake, which she called Harry Dean Stanton.

At the June 2000 Los Angeles premiere of *Gone in 60 Seconds*, Angelina with her second husband, Billy Bob Thornton. She had his name tattooed on her left biceps – it has since been lasered off.

In the role Lara Croft, which put her into the $10-million-a-picture bracket, with her padded 36Ds.
Tomb Raider: The Cradle of Life [2003]
c.Paramount/Everett/ REX FEATURES

Known in the film industry for being a tough nut, Angelina does most of her own stunts.

Snowdonia, Wales set for *Tomb Raider*, Sept 2000.

Huw Evans/ REX FEATURES

Sept 2004: Los Angeles
premiere of *Sky Captain and
the World of Tomorrow*. While
signing autographs Angelina
was startled by a gatecrasher.
Jim Smeal/BEI/ REX FEATURES

Cambodian Maddox with his mum on
the merry-go-round in Central Park,
New York, in June 2005.
Alecsey Boldeskull/ REX FEATURES

In the delightful *Mr. & Mrs. Smith*, Angelina with her next husband, Brad Pitt, whom she 'did not ͏g' on set in January 2005. Some might not believe her but she is a lady who tells it like it is.
20th Century Fox/ REX FEATURES

ͻve] Beefcake Brad was quickly housetrained...well, as they say in Hollywood, pussywhippped into ͷnging nappies and being nanny. He is carrying Angelina's second adopted child, Sahara, whose ͻpian parents died of AIDS. They are coming through customs at Nice airport, March 2006.
Press/ REX FEATURES

One of the proudest moments in Angelina's acting career
– at the 2000 Oscars she takes Best Actress in a Supporting
Role for her portrayal of Lisa Rowe in *Girl, Interrupted*
Stewart Cook/ REX FEATURES

Always eager to flash her tattoos, Angelina sits for a portrait in 2003, which shows how Billy Bob was lasered off her arm and out of her life.
John Taylor/ REX FEATURES

[below] While appearing on American TV in March 2004, Angelina flashes her latest tattoo, on her upper back: 'Know your rights'. She treats her body like it was a T-shirt.

Angelina at a UNHCR press
conference in Moscow in Aug 2003
Sipa Press/ REX FEATURES